NOTES

English- Language Arts

ADVANTAGE CAHSEE

California High School

KAPLAN

K12 LEARNING
SERVICES

Developed by

Andrew Ordover, Joanna Cohen

ELL Annotations

Laurie Blass, HEURISTIX

Editors

Jenny Weiss, Abby Remer, Charli Engelhorn, Chandra Thomas

Cover

Maurice Kessler

Design

Pamela Beaulieu

Production

Baly Lau, Alisa Caratozzolo, Scott Rayow

Illustration

Erika Quiroz

Director of Curriculum and Instruction

Deborah Lerman

Table of Contents

Mini Practice Test

Mini Practice Test

This unit contains a sample CAHSEE in English-Language Arts.

This is not the actual CAHSEE, so don't worry! This is simply a practice test. Your performance will not be graded or scored. The test will give you a brief taste of the CAHSEE, and will give your teacher a sense of your strengths and weaknesses in areas likely to be tested, so that you can get the help you need between now and test day.

So relax, have fun, and do your best. This is just one step on your climb to the summit of CAHSEE success.

Sample CAHSEE
English-Language Arts

This test contains several reading passages, 19 multiple-choice questions, and one essay question. You will have one hour to complete the test.

When your teacher tells you to start, you may turn the page and begin working.

Read the following article, and answer questions 1–5.

A Brief History of Coins

Most of us don't think about the change in our pockets or purses, but those coins have a fascinating history that can teach us a lot about our own culture and other cultures throughout history.

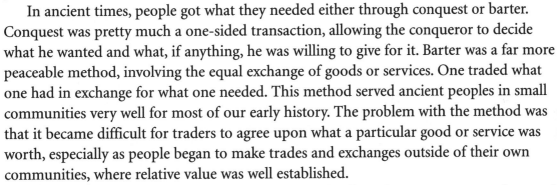

Coin collecting is a popular hobby in many countries and has been for many years. People have been collecting coins as long as there have been coins. Coins provide a fascinating window into history. Each one is a miniature work of art, reflecting its historical era and the culture from which it originated. Coins can tell us, in concentrated form, what a particular group of people in a particular place at a particular time held sacred and important.

In ancient times, people got what they needed either through conquest or barter. Conquest was pretty much a one-sided transaction, allowing the conqueror to decide what he wanted and what, if anything, he was willing to give for it. Barter was a far more peaceable method, involving the equal exchange of goods or services. One traded what one had in exchange for what one needed. This method served ancient peoples in small communities very well for most of our early history. The problem with the method was that it became difficult for traders to agree upon what a particular good or service was worth, especially as people began to make trades and exchanges outside of their own communities, where relative value was well established.

Another problem with barter arose as towns and villages became more populous and travel between them became more routine. Certain goods were extremely difficult to transport, especially over the long distances that the more adventurous traders were beginning to attempt. Some goods and many services were *impossible* to transport. If commerce was to reach beyond the limits of the village square, what was needed was some form of common currency—some unit of trade that was agreed on by all people in a particular region and was easily transportable.

Metals became the obvious choice. Because of their usefulness in fashioning a variety of desirable objects, from knives to cooking pots, they were valuable to everyone in a community. They were also strong enough to move from hand to hand without falling apart. The value of goods and services could be defined in terms of their weight in gold, or silver, or other precious metals available in the region.

We do not know who first decided to stamp designs on metal to make them into coins, but it probably happened somewhere in Asia Minor during the 7th Century B.C. The earliest coins we have come from Lydia and Ionia, which are now in western Turkey. The ancient Greeks, Persians, and Romans all minted coins of silver, gold, and bronze.

Each coin was cast to a certain, agreed-upon weight. It was then heated to make it soft and was struck with a hammer between two engraved dies. Surviving examples of these early coins usually show a symbol of the city or its ruler on one side and a simple mark on the other side. These are considered the first true coins of the world, because they were composed of a scarce and valuable metal, had a consistent weight, and were guaranteed by the ruler of the area.

The idea of coin currency quickly spread to the islands and city-states of western Greece. It was here during Greece's Golden Age that master engravers turned simple units of currency into small works of art. The gods of the Greek pantheon were depicted with as much beauty as possible to extol the Greek ideals of beauty and perfection.

As Alexander the Great (336–323 B.C.) swept across southern Europe, he brought the concept of coinage with him. Coins were minted with realistic portraits of Alexander and his generals and successors. These coins became the currency of a great empire.

The Roman Empire continued this tradition of realistic portraiture. Roman coins glorified not only the rulers, but also their accomplishments—the cities they built, the military campaigns they waged, and so on. Much of what we know of these rulers comes from the coins they had minted in their own honor. History often has cause to be grateful for the egotism of monarchs.

With the rise of Christianity during the reign of the emperor Constantine (A.D. 307–337), heavenly rulers and religious scenes replaced human rulers on the coins of the realm. The gold coin of that era, called the *solidus*, was used from Constantine's time through the Middle Ages for a period of nearly one thousand years.

In our own time, human faces have again taken center stage. George Washington objected to the idea of having his face on American coins, thinking that it was a dangerous step towards monarchy. In spite of his fears, however, his face and that of President Lincoln began appearing on American coins by 1899. Today, presidents from Roosevelt to Kennedy grace many of our coins.

As you can see, the coins jingling in your pocket are not just small change. They are pieces of history and steps in a long process of cultural evolution. The most commonplace things can often connect us with exotic people, places, and times.

1. **Which of the following is NOT true of the *solidus*?**

   A   It was made of gold.

   B   It made use of religious imagery.

   C   It was used for almost a thousand years.

   D   It celebrated the reign of Constantine.

2. **Read this sentence from the article.**

   > Another problem with barter arose as towns and villages became more populous and travel between them became more routine.

   As it is used here, what does *routine* mean?

   A   boring

   B   unpredictable

   C   disciplined

   D   common

3. **Which of the following is an example of barter?**

   A   mowing someone's lawn for piano lessons

   B   serving food at a local homeless shelter

   C   working in a local doctor's office after school

   D   visiting a friend or relative in a neighboring town

4. **Which sentence from the passage BEST summarizes the author's main point?**

   A   Coins provide a fascinating window into history.

   B   People have been collecting coins as long as there have been coins.

   C   These coins became the currency of a great empire.

   D   The value of goods and services could be defined in terms of their weight in gold, or silver, or other precious metals available in the region.

5. **When the author says, "History often has cause to be grateful for the egotism of monarchs," she MOST LIKELY means that—**

   A   proud, selfish men have often been very effective at leading human societies.

   B   much of what we know of the ancient world comes from the self-praise of rulers.

   C   history is driven forward by the desires and appetites of arrogant leaders.

   D   historians enjoy studying dominant, larger-than-life political figures.

Read the passage and answer questions 6–10.

Dimitri's Big Day

Dimitri reclined on his unmade bed and thought of the afternoon that had just ended. Even after months of intense preparation, he could hardly believe that he had finally done it. He had completed his first solo flight as a licensed private pilot!

The flight had seemed short, although he knew it had lasted well over an hour. Dimitri had arrived at the local airport at nine in the morning. Because he was so nervous about his test flight, he wanted to spend as much time as he could with the airplane he was about to fly. He pulled out the special cleaning solvent, horsehair brush, and light wax from the supply shed in the hangar and began to wash and then polish the small single-engine plane. His brush moved in circular patterns along the top and bottom of each wing. Dimitri removed some debris that had collected in the creases along the fin. He wanted to make sure that the plane was absolutely spotless when he embarked on his first solo voyage. By the time Dimitri's instructor, Zaidy, arrived on the tarmac, Dimitri had been there for nearly three hours.

Just before taking off, Dimitri took a deep breath and said to himself, "Okay, here we go!"

Dimitri's mind had been fully engaged during the entire flight, constantly analyzing the plane's position in the air, as well as scolding himself for his slight mistakes. As he was taking off, the wing flaps of the plane had hitched a little. Dimitri knew this was a common error for young pilots. He hoped that Zaidy, who watched from the ground, had not noticed, or that she would not penalize him too harshly for his small mistake.

Dimitri soared above his small, sleepy town, gliding through the air in the freshly waxed plane.

But now, relaxing in his room, Dimitri's mind was occupied by other, more mundane thoughts.

The hums of Dimitri's family dancing through their early evening rituals drifted into his otherwise tranquil bedroom. His younger sister, Helena, was in her room gabbing on the phone and messaging on the computer with several of her friends. It seemed Helena could turn the littlest thing into endless hours of gossip with her friends. His little brother, Marcus, was in his room, squashing the many minions of the cyber-world while vigorously pressing the video-game controller. His dad was downstairs trying to figure out what to make for dinner. Dimitri hoped that he would decide to order delivery from the Mexican restaurant down the block.

Ordinarily, Dimitri would have been watching his favorite program on TV or thinking about his newspaper route. However, tonight he was content to simply lie on his bed and relive the glorious experiences of the afternoon. The fact that Dimitri could share his excitement about the afternoon's events with his dad made it even better.

Dimitri's dad was a commercial airline pilot. His father, Dimitri's grandfather, had been a pilot in World War II flying B-24 Liberators. Dimitri's dad had not entered the military, but he was an experienced pilot, both in the commercial and private realms.

Along with four other pilots, Dimitri's dad owned a share of a Cessna 172. The four-seater airplane could accommodate family members and friends, and he had been taking them for pleasure flights for as long as Dimitri could remember.

Dimitri had instantly become enamored. He loved to fly. Immediately after that flight with his father, Dimitri raced to the library to take out every book he could find about flying and airplanes. From his research, he had learned he could start taking pilot lessons, and, if he performed well, get his student license at 16. Then, when he was 17, he would be able to get his full pilot's license and even carry passengers, which would definitely impress his classmates and teachers at school.

So, for the past 18 months, Dimitri had worked diligently after school and on weekends, delivering papers and mowing lawns so that he could afford flight lessons from Zaidy, who was a certified instructor. He would also have to earn enough money to pay for his share of fuel and maintenance on the group plane in order to take his hard-earned place at the controls. During all that time, Dimitri knew that the extra effort was worth it. Once he became a pilot, his life would change. He would be different, and others would see him differently. He would be mature and proud, having worked hard to achieve something very special. He would gain the respect of his peers and adults alike in that wonderful, shining moment when he received his pilot's license. He was confident that he would never be seen as a child again.

Well, now his dream had become a reality. His big day had finally arrived—he was a licensed pilot. He clasped his hands behind his head, looked up at the clouds painted on his otherwise unpretentious bedroom ceiling, and basked in the warm glow of adulthood. His smile was the contented smile of a man who had just accomplished a lifelong goal.

Suddenly, his father called up the stairs, "Dimitri, come down here. It's your turn to take out the trash!"

In those two sentences, Dimitri came back to reality. He knew that he could become a pilot, or achieve any number of important, grown-up ambitions, but that somehow he would always be his father's son.

6. **Which of the following is the main theme of the passage?**

    A   Determination leads to disappointment.

    B   One achievement can impress everyone.

    C   Dreams are impossible to accomplish.

    D   Responsibilities are part of adulthood.

7. **Which organizational pattern does the author use in this passage?**

    A   The author uses a chronological story that is interrupted by flashbacks.

    B   The author uses an article that compares and contrasts Dimitri and his siblings.

    C   The author uses chronological fiction interrupted by long descriptions.

    D   The author uses descriptive nonfiction of one event through many points of view.

8. **Which sentence from the passage is an example of figurative language?**

    A   He had completed his first solo flight as a licensed private pilot!

    B   The hums of Dimitri's family dancing through their early evening rituals drifted into his otherwise tranquil bedroom.

    C   Immediately after that flight with his father, Dimitri raced to the library to take out every book he could find about flying and airplanes.

    D   During all that time, Dimitri knew that the extra effort was worth it.

9. **Which of the following BEST summarizes the main details of the passage?**

    A   A young man follows in his father's footsteps.

    B   Passing a solo-flight test fails to change a young man's life.

    C   A young man dreams of taking his family and friends for a ride.

    D   A solo flight becomes a step in growing up for a young man.

10. **As a pilot, Dimitri would BEST be described as—**

    A   underappreciated.

    B   overenthusiastic.

    C   detail-oriented.

    D   uninterested.

Choose the answer that is the most effective substitute for each underlined part of the sentence. If no substitution is necessary, choose "Leave as is."

11. **Carlos knew his way around the woods, even in the dark. <u>Otherwise, he would have been nervous about being alone in the dark. With wild animals lurking nearby.</u>**

   A   Otherwise, he would have been nervous about being alone in the dark; wild animals lurking nearby.

   B   Otherwise, he would have been nervous about being alone in the dark, wild animals were lurking nearby.

   C   Otherwise, he would have been nervous about being alone in the dark with wild animals lurking nearby.

   D   Leave as is.

12. **The reporters were eager to attend <u>the trial in the small town of the spies.</u>**

   A   the trial of the spies in the small town.

   B   the trial at the small town of the spies.

   C   in the small town, the trial of the spies.

   D   Leave as is.

13. **The instructions state quite clearly that <u>when the test booklets are handed out by the teacher, students should sit quietly</u> and stop talking.**

   A   when the teacher has been handing out the test booklets, students should sit quietly

   B   when the teacher hands out the test booklets, students should sit quietly

   C   when the test booklets are handed out by the teacher and students should sit quietly

   D   Leave as is.

Choose the word or phrase that best completes the sentence.

14. **Neither the president nor the congress _____ the power to declare a law unconstitutional.**

   A   has

   B   have

   C   having

   D   could have

15. **_____ Albert Einstein declared, "is more important than knowledge."**

   A   "Imagination"

   B   "Imagination,

   C   "Imagination,"

   D   Imagination

The following is a rough draft of an essay that discusses the history of a world-famous art museum. It may contain errors in grammar, punctuation, sentence structure, and organization. Some of the questions may refer to underlined or numbered sentences or phrases within the text. Read the essay and answer questions 16–19.

(1) Located on the bank of the Seine River in Paris, France, it is home to over 250,000 works of art. (2) Included among the large number of paintings, sculptures, and other items are some of the most famous works in history. (3) Both the Mona Lisa and the Venus de Milo <u>are making their home at the Louvre</u>.

(4) Originally constructed in 1190 as a fortress for King Philip. (5) The Louvre later became the residence of the King. (6) This magnificent building was so large that the King and his son used to ride on horseback through the halls. (7) But in 1793, after the French Revolution, the French Republic established the museum, and the Louvre was opened up for all people to see art.

(8) In 1981, French President Mitterand launched a project to expand the Louvre.

(9) A special area was designated for each of the seven departments that house the art collections.

(10) The Egyptian Antiquities department is home to a large granite Sphinx. (11) The Asian Antiquities department contains ancient Chinese sculptures. (12) Venus de Milo resides in the department of Greek, Etruscan, and Roman Antiquities. (13) The Paintings department holds a fine selection of works by well-known art masters. (14) Special objects of artistic merit, such as tapestries and historical items, reside in a special area.

(15) French Sculpture is particularly well represented and has an area all its own. (16) The final department is that of Graphic Art, which includes drawings, prints, and watercolors.

(17) The Louvre is one of the world's most important museums. (18) It reflects the <u>centuries for</u> political and social change that reformed the face of history. (19) It has become a well-loved refuge for artists and art lovers.

16. **Which sentence would BEST begin the essay?**

    A   Many people visit the art museum the Louvre each year.

    B   The Louvre is one of the largest museums in the world.

    C   You will read about the Louvre in this paper.

    D   Museums are interesting places to visit.

17. **Which change to the underlined clause in sentence 3 would make it more consistent with the first part of the sentence?**

    A   make their home at the Louvre

    B   somehow make a home at the Louvre

    C   have made their home at the Louvre

    D   Leave as is.

18. **What is the BEST way to combine the sentences labeled 4 and 5?**

    A   The Louvre later became the King's residence so it was originally constructed in 1190 as a fortress for King Philip.

    B   In 1190 the Louvre was a fortress for King Philip, later becoming a residence.

    C   The King's residence was constructed in 1190 as a fortress for King Philip.

    D   Originally constructed in 1190 as a fortress for King Philip, the Louvre later became the King's residence.

19. **Which phrase would BEST replace the underlined phrase in sentence 18?**

    A   centuries with

    B   centuries by

    C   centuries of

    D   Leave as is.

Writing Task:

Standardized high school exit examinations like the CAHSEE have been in the news across the country for several years. Some people believe they are accurate and useful assessments that can provide colleges and parents with valuable information on the student and the school's academic program; other people argue that the tests are inauthentic assessments that waste valuable school time and provide limited and inaccurate information.

Write a composition stating and defending your position on standardized high school exit exams.

Checklist for Your Writing

The following checklist will help you do your best work. Make sure you:

☐ Read the task carefully.

☐ Use specific details and examples to demonstrate your understanding.

☐ Organize your writing with a strong introduction, body, and conclusion.

☐ Choose a style, tone, and vocabulary that are appropriate for your audience and purpose.

☐ Vary your sentences to make your writing interesting to read.

☐ Check for mistakes in grammar, spelling, punctuation, and sentence structure.

_____

_____

_____

_____

_____

_____

_____

unit

1

SEEING THE BIG PICTURE

Thinking KAP

1. What is your favorite movie?

   _____

2. Why is it your favorite?

   _____

3. What is the movie about?

   _____

   _____

   _____

   _____

   _____

4. If you were trying to convince a friend to see this movie, what else would you want to tell him?

   _____

   _____

   _____

   _____

   _____

   _____

The Big Picture

Multiple-choice questions on the CAHSEE will often ask you about "big picture" issues related to reading passages. Big picture issues include things like the main idea, the author's purpose and point of view, and the overall theme or message.

Being able to identify the main idea of something is very important. When our friends ask us about a book we have read or a movie we have seen, we don't want to spend all day telling them every single detail. They just want the basics—the big picture.

But how do we know what the big picture *is*?

The Fortune Cookie
The main idea of any story—even a long novel—should be short enough to fit inside a fortune cookie.

Reading for the 2Ws

The simplest way to get to the heart of a reading passage is to identify the 2Ws: The **Who** and the **What**.

The **Who** is the subject of the passage.

Ask yourself this question: "Who is this passage about?"

The **What** is the action of the passage.

Ask yourself this question: "What does the Who do?"

Who + **What** should give you a clear, simple statement of the main idea.

Here is an example from a famous movie:

Who is the movie about?   Spider-Man

What does the **Who** do?   Saves the city

Main Idea: Spider-Man saves the city.

Try It Out!

Read the paragraph below. Identify the 2Ws and state the main idea.

   The poems of the earliest Greeks were intended to be sung or recited, not written down, because they were created before the Greeks began to use writing for literary purposes. The poets (called "bards") remembered the poems by reciting the lines over and over again. Also, some of the stories were improvised—the poets invented the plots on the spot. Because the poems were never recorded, all that remains of them today are fragments mentioned by later Greek writers.

Who is the passage about? _____

What does the Who do? _____

Main Idea: _____

Just Enough
Don't get nervous when you notice how much information you are leaving out. A main idea gives a *general* or overall sense of something.

Predicting

Distracting Answer Choices

Answer choices for multiple-choice questions often look good for one reason or another but are incorrect. If you aren't absolutely certain about your answer, you might fall for these distracting, appealing answers. Even when you do know the answer, you can be led astray by choices that look tempting.

Making Predictions

An important strategy for avoiding wrong answer choices on multiple-choice questions is Predicting. Before even looking at the answer choices, you should predict what the correct answer should be.

Predicting
• Cover the answer choices before reading the question.
• Read the question and predict what the answer will be.
• Find the choice that most closely matches your prediction.

Cover the Choices
You should physically cover the answer choices with your hand. That way you won't be tempted to look at them when you predict.

Try It Out!

Here is a typical main-idea question. The correct answer has been left out. Can you use your knowledge of the 2Ws to fill it in?

1. **The main idea of this passage is that the poems of the earliest Greeks were—**

   A   accompanied by musical instruments.

   B   translated by modern Greek writers.

   C   meticulously recorded on paper.

   D   _____

▷ Why isn't (A) correct?   _____

▷ Why isn't (B) correct?   _____

▷ Why isn't (C) correct?   _____

Eliminate Extremes
Extreme language includes words such as *never, always, none, all, best,* and *worst.*

Another powerful strategy for multiple-choice questions is Eliminating. When you eliminate answer choices, you increase your chances of choosing the correct answer. Fill in the chart below.

# of Choices Eliminated	Chance of Guessing the Answer
0	25%
1	_____
2	_____
3	_____

The Author's Purpose

Some main-idea questions will ask you to determine the author's purpose in writing a passage or the author's attitude towards the topic.

You do not have to be a mind reader to figure this out. Good writers labor over every aspect of what they do, from the choice of topics to the choice of individual words, because every aspect of their writing helps them communicate their ideas and feelings.

Uncovering the Author's Purpose in Informational Passages

Nonfiction tends to be pretty straightforward and informational. Often it tells you exactly *why* it's telling you something. Your job will be to figure out why the author wants you to know it.

As you read, ask yourself these questions:

- What does the author want me to know about the topic?
- Why is it important that I know this?
- What does the author want me to do with this knowledge?

▷ Why might an author write a newspaper editorial?

Uncovering the Author's Purpose in Literary Passages

The purpose or point of view of fiction can be trickier to figure out, but it's not impossible. Look at the major elements of the story and ask yourself, "Why?"

- Why did the author choose this character to be the main character?
- Why does the story take place where it does?
- Why does the story take place when it does?
- Why does the main character do what s/he does?

▷ Whose point of view is expressed in your favorite movie?

Look Under the Hood
Think like a mechanic. After all, writing doesn't just happen; it has to be *made*. Think about *how* it was made and what parts went into making it.

Try It Out!

Read this narrative passage, and answer the questions below.

The Kite Flyer

Dario loved flying kites. Ever since he'd flown his first kite at age 8, he had made and flown every kind of kite he could find. He got a paper route so that he could buy more kites.

One particularly windy day, Dario was flying his favorite kite. Running down a hill to keep his kite in the air, he fell and broke his leg. The doctor said he would be in bed for several weeks and then on crutches for a long time. His mother told him kite-flying was out of the question. He longed to be outside, watching kites swoop and swerve like big beautiful birds.

Dario began to doodle in a notebook. He sketched his favorite kite. Suddenly he had an idea. It took several weeks, but he taught himself to draw very detailed pictures of different kinds of kites. He began to think about how kites were designed. Just as he was ready to start hobbling around on crutches, he had an idea for a kite that would be better than any he had built so far.

Dario hobbled to the window. He could see several kites flying. Soon he would be out there again. In the meantime, he had a kite to make. The time would swoop and swerve right by him.

What Does It All Mean?
If a question asks you about the deeper meaning or lesson, think about how the **What** has changed the **Who** by the end of the story.

First ask:

▷ Why did the author choose Dario to be the main character?

_____

▷ Why does the story take place when and where it does?

_____

▷ Why does Dario do what he does?

_____

Then answer:

1. What does the author think of Dario?

_____

2. What was the author's purpose in writing this story?

_____

Guided Practice

The Hudson River School

Read Like Goldilocks
When looking for a main idea, remember not to be too broad or too narrow. Your main idea should hit the middle and be "just right."

The first truly American art movement was formed by a group of landscape painters that emerged in the early 19th century called the Hudson River School. The first works in this style were created by Thomas Cole, Thomas Doughty, and Asher Durand, a trio of painters who worked from approximately 1835 to 1870 in the Hudson River Valley and surrounding locations.

Heavily influenced by European Romanticism, these painters set out to convey the splendor of the American wilderness. The strongly nationalistic tone of their paintings caught the spirit of the times, and within a generation the movement had mushroomed to include landscape painters from all over the United States.

One factor contributing to the success of the Hudson River School was the rapid growth of American nationalism in the early 19th century. The War of 1812 had given the United States a new sense of pride in its identity, and as the nation continued to grow, there was a desire to compete with Europe on both economic and cultural grounds.

The vast panoramas of the Hudson River School fit the bill perfectly by providing a new movement in art that was unmistakably American in origin. Canvases celebrating such typically American scenes as Niagara Falls, Boston Harbor, and the expansion of the railroad into rural Pennsylvania were greeted with enormous popular acclaim.

Who is the passage about? _____

What does the **Who** do?_____

Main Idea: _____

1. **Which of the following MOST accurately indicates the author's feelings about the painters of the Hudson River School?**

    A They blindly accepted the established rules of painting.

    B They were excellent imitators of European paintings.

    C They alerted America to the dangers of urban development.

    D They appealed to the patriotic sentiments of their age.

Independent Practice

Read this selection from Helen Keller's memoirs, and answer the questions that follow.

from
The Story of My Life

by HELEN KELLER

One day my teacher and I were returning from a long ramble. The morning had been fine, but it was growing warm and sultry when at last we turned our faces homeward. Two or three times we stopped to rest under a tree by the wayside. Our last halt was under a wild cherry tree a short distance from the house. The shade was grateful, and the tree was so easy to climb that with my teacher's assistance I was able to scramble to a seat in the branches. It was so cool up in the tree that Miss Sullivan proposed that we have our luncheon there. I promised to keep still while she went to the house to fetch it. Suddenly a change passed over the tree. All the sun's warmth left the air. I knew the sky was black, because all the heat, which meant light to me, had died out of the atmosphere. A strange odor came up from the earth. I knew it, it was the odor that always precedes a thunderstorm, and a nameless fear clutched at my heart. I felt absolutely alone, cut off from my friends and the firm earth. The immense, the unknown, enfolded me. I remained still and expectant; a chilling terror crept over me. I longed for my teacher's return; but above all things I wanted to get down from that tree.

There was a moment of sinister silence, then a multitudinous stirring of the leaves. A shiver ran through the tree, and the wind sent forth a blast that would have knocked me off had I not clung to the branch with might and main. The tree swayed and strained. The small twigs snapped and fell about me in showers. A wild impulse to jump seized me, but terror held me fast. I crouched down in the fork of the tree. The branches lashed about me. I felt the intermittent jarring that came now and then, as if something heavy had fallen and the shock had traveled up till it reached the limb I sat on. It worked my suspense up to the highest point, and just as I was thinking the tree and I should fall together, my teacher seized my hand and helped me down. I clung to her, trembling with joy to feel the earth under my feet once more. It is true what they say, that nature "wages open war against her children, and under softest touch hides treacherous claws."

1. **What is the main purpose of Keller's story?**

    A   to explain the author's lifelong fear of
        the outdoors

    B   to describe the author's terrifying and
        lonely childhood

    C   to illustrate how the author learned the
        truth about nature

    D   to argue against allowing children to
        climb trees by themselves

    HINT The main idea should not be
    too broad or too narrow.

2. **Which sentence from the story BEST
    illustrates what Helen Keller learns from
    this episode?**

    A   "Nature wages open war against her
        children, and under softest touch hides
        treacherous claws."

    B   "I longed for my teacher's return; but
        above all things I wanted to get down
        from that tree."

    C   "I felt absolutely alone, cut off from my
        friends and the firm earth."

    D   "I clung to her, trembling with joy
        to feel the earth under my feet once
        more."

    HINT How does the What change
    the Who during the story?

3. **Which word BEST describes Helen Keller's
    opinion of this childhood adventure?**

    A   haunting

    B   triumphant

    C   treacherous

    D   educational

    HINT Which answer choice reflects
    the author's opinion
    throughout the story?

Test Practice

Read this passage, and answer questions 1–4.

All About the Benjamin

> Although Benjamin Franklin had little formal schooling, his curiosity and inventiveness made him one of the most important founding fathers.

Benjamin Franklin was a patriot, a diplomat, an author, a printer, a scientist, and an inventor. He researched electricity and invented the lightning rod. He created the first bifocal glasses and the Franklin stove. He was a signer of the Declaration of Independence and helped to develop the Constitution of the United States. He even invented a combination desk and chair, which many students still use in their schools.

Unlike so many people these days, Franklin didn't feel he had to be just one thing or have just one job. Franklin had only two years of formal schooling, but he spent his lifetime learning new facts, developing new skills, and discovering new ways of doing things. A true Renaissance man of the Enlightenment era, Benjamin Franklin found something interesting in every part of the world and made important contributions in many, many fields.

Franklin was born in 1706, the 15th child of a Boston soap and candle maker. At the age of 10, young Franklin was apprenticed to his father, but he didn't enjoy candle making. After two years, he was apprenticed to his brother James, who was a printer. James had started the *The New England Courant*, the first truly American newspaper, reporting news from the colonies to the colonies. Benjamin's apprenticeship with James lasted five years. During that time, Franklin taught himself the classics and worked to improve his writing style. He secretly contributed humorous letters of advice and criticism to his brother's newspaper, pretending to be an old widow named Silence Dogood. The "Dogood" letters became a huge hit, and people demanded to know who this mystery woman was. Franklin eventually admitted that he had written them, earning himself a reputation—and the anger of his older brother.

While sharpening his wit and his writing skills, the young Franklin also worked to make himself morally perfect.

Young people today may laugh at such a project, but Benjamin Franklin took it seriously. He made himself a little red book in which he listed what he considered to be the most important human virtues. He used the book to keep track of his moral progress, noting when he had been good and when he had fallen short of his goals.

In his *Autobiography*, Franklin listed some of the goals he had set for himself as a young man.

1. TEMPERANCE. Eat not to dullness; drink not to elevation.
2. SILENCE. Speak not but what may benefit others or yourself; avoid trifling conversation.
3. ORDER. Let all your things have their places; let each part of your business have its time.
4. RESOLUTION. Resolve to perform what you ought; perform without fail what you resolve.
5. FRUGALITY. Make no expense but to do good to others or yourself; i.e., waste nothing.
6. INDUSTRY. Lose no time; be always employ'd in something useful; cut off all unnecessary actions.
7. SINCERITY. Use no hurtful deceit; think innocently and justly, and, if you speak, speak accordingly.
8. JUSTICE. Wrong none by doing injuries, or omitting the benefits that are your duty.
9. MODERATION. Avoid extreams; forbear resenting injuries so much as you think they deserve.
10. CLEANLINESS. Tolerate no uncleanliness in body, cloaths, or habitation.

Benjamin Franklin had his faults and shortcomings, like any human being. He may not have been successful at perfecting himself, but he certainly managed to make himself into an accomplished and admired man. Not only did he become a successful printer and author, he also started the first public library in America, the first volunteer fire department, and the Academy of Philadelphia, which eventually became the University of Pennsylvania. He was sent to England to represent the American colonies and was later appointed to the Second Continental Congress, where he helped to draft the Declaration of Independence. He also participated in the Constitutional Convention, where his ability to mediate and forge compromises among disparate parties proved crucial in getting our Constitution drafted and ratified. In so many ways, the birth of our nation depended on Franklin's wise, guiding hand.

Benjamin Franklin never stopped working, learning, and experimenting. At the age of 71, he was sent to France to negotiate treaties for the new American republic. One of his final public acts, at the age of 84, was to sign a petition urging the United States Congress to abolish slavery.

Franklin had come a long way from the young man who kept track of his virtues and faults in a little red book. He may not have achieved the perfection he sought as a young man, but what he *did* achieve, few others have equaled.

1. This passage is MOSTLY about Benjamin Franklin's—

   A childhood.

   B virtues.

   C inventions.

   D accomplishments.

2. What is the main purpose of this biographical essay?

   A to persuade you to imitate Benjamin Franklin

   B to educate you about Benjamin Franklin's life and work

   C to amuse you with stories about Benjamin Franklin's youth

   D to warn you to set goals for yourself in life

3. Which of the following sentences from the passage MOST accurately indicates the author's attitude toward Benjamin Franklin?

   A "Benjamin Franklin had his faults and shortcomings, like any human being."

   B "Franklin never stopped working, learning, and experimenting."

   C "Franklin taught himself the classics and worked to improve his writing style."

   D "Benjamin Franklin is considered to be one of the founding fathers of the United States."

4. According to this author, what is the BEST lesson we can learn from Benjamin Franklin's life?

   A The key to a successful life is to be morally perfect.

   B It is wise not to do to any one thing for too many years.

   C Being interested in many things can keep you young and vital.

   D People are no longer as well educated as the founding fathers were.

Unit 1 ReKAP

Look back at the strategies in this unit and review them. Then, fill in the spaces below to show what you have learned.

- When reading passages for the main idea, I will look for the W_____ and

  the W_____.

- To understand the author's purpose in writing an informational passage, I will

  ask myself what the author wants me to _____ about the topic, and why

  the author thinks it is _____.

- To understand the author's purpose in writing a literary passage, I will ask

  myself why the main character _____.

- I will use _____ and _____ to help me identify correct

  answers and avoid incorrect answers on multiple-choice questions.

READING NONFICTION PASSAGES

Thinking KAP

Create a set of directions from this school to your home. Make the directions as clear and unambiguous as possible. Use any writing or graphic strategies you think will add clarity to your directions.

Types of Nonfiction Texts

The CAHSEE includes a wide variety of nonfiction texts, from essays to biographies to workplace documents. What all of these texts have in common is that they are based on facts and are concerned with real-life situations or problems.

What makes these texts different from each other is the author's purpose. Each type of nonfiction text has a specific purpose—a specific reason for being. Two writers may both write about ants, but if one is writing a science text and another is writing an editorial, their purposes and approaches will be very different.

Try It Out!

Describe each type of nonfiction writing, and explain its purpose.

Persuasive Essay/Newspaper Editorial

▷ Description: _____

▷ Purpose: _____

Science Article

▷ Description: _____

▷ Purpose: _____

History Article

▷ Description: _____

▷ Purpose: _____

Biography

▷ Description: _____

▷ Purpose: _____

Procedures/Instructions

▷ Description: _____

▷ Purpose: _____

Brochure/Advertisement

▷ Description: _____

▷ Purpose: _____

Detail Questions

Nonfiction texts try to present information or arguments clearly and effectively. Multiple-choice questions about nonfiction texts will often focus on the facts and details being presented, asking **what, which, when, where, why,** and **how** questions.

Here are some typical examples of detail-oriented questions.

1. Which of the following is NOT discussed in the brochure?

2. Scientists include a control in every experiment because—

3. According to the chart in the document, what is the BEST diet to feed a parrot?

4. Which sentence from the article explains specifically how to...?

Some **why** questions will require you to read between the lines and use your judgment and reasoning skills to find an answer. We will discuss inference questions like these in a later unit.

For today, we are concerned with the facts and details that are actually presented in the text.

Try It Out!

List the five most important details from the passage about Benjamin Franklin that appeared in Unit 1.

_____

_____

_____

_____

_____

What makes those the **most** important details?

_____

_____

The 4-Step Method for Reading Comprehension

Reading passages can be long, dense, and time consuming. Kaplan's 4-Step Method gives you a systematic way to approach reading passages so that you can use your time most effectively. This method enables you to use the test questions and the 2Ws to find the most important details—the ones you will need to answer the questions.

The Keys to the Kingdom
You will be seeing this 4-Step Method again as we work through the test. It is the key to reading efficiently on tests. Learn it!

The 4-Step Method for Reading Comprehension
STEP 1 Scan the questions first.
STEP 2 Read for the 2Ws.
STEP 3 Read each paragraph for important information.
STEP 4 Return to the questions and answer them.

Try It Out!

Making chili is not an exact science. Don't expect to find lists of items and perfectly-measured amounts here. Chili is a matter of taste and experience. Chili is art. Chili is also personal. Many people will disagree with my approach, some quite heatedly. But this is my chili, not theirs. It may not be a 4-star recipe, or even a 4-alarm recipe, but it is simple, fun, and delicious, and you're guaranteed to get a great meal out of it.

Why does the author say that making chili is an art?

_____

▷ What do you learn by scanning the question?

_____

▷ What is the main idea?

_____

▷ What important information in the paragraph will help you answer the question?

_____

Don't Jump!
Never jump to a conclusion. It's always best to find evidence for any answer.

Dig for Details

You know what details are, and you know why they are important. However, finding details can often be very time-consuming. It's easy to get bogged down in details and lose sight of the big picture.

Make sure to read the passage only for *important* information, not for every piece of information the author gives you. You want to get a sense of the main idea and then underline the details that support it. Don't get weighed down trying to underline or memorize every single detail. It's not worth your time, and it won't help you answer the questions.

When you reach Step 4, you may find that you can answer some questions very quickly, without having to look back at the text. If so—great!

However, you may find that for some questions you need to go back into the passage and read more closely. Perhaps you underlined an important detail, but it doesn't give you the answer to the question. That's fine. Take the time to do research and close reading *where you need it.*

Doing research in a passage is called Digging for Details.

- **Identify** the detail needed to answer the question.
- **Find** the first mention of the detail in the text.
- **Closely read** the sentence **before** the mention of the detail.
- **Closely read** the sentence **containing** the detail.
- **Closely read** the sentence **after** the mention of the detail.

If Digging for Details does not give you the answer you need, go back and **widen your search**. Read two sentences surrounding the detail. If that doesn't work, try three. In most cases, the facts you need for detail-oriented questions will be fairly close to the detail itself.

Wider Lens

Digging for Details will not work on Big Picture questions, fact or inference questions about the main idea or the lesson. For those questions, you will need an understanding of the entire passage.

Try It Out!

Every step of making chili varies according to the chef. I say start early in the morning so that it has time to cook all day. Others make it a day ahead; they think it acquires better taste over time. I say you can have too much of a good thing! One day is plenty.

First dump a couple of cans of crushed tomatoes or a couple of handfuls of freshly cut tomatoes into a slow-cooker or a large pot on a low flame. Sauté a panful of onions and some garlic. I say "some garlic" because everyone has his or her own preference. I like a lot—an entire head.

Dump the onions and garlic into the pot, and sauté a panful of diced green peppers with a few jalapeños or other hot peppers thrown in to taste. Dump those in the pot, and then use the same pan to brown some meat. Some people like chopped meat; I prefer cubed steak. Don't cook it all the way through, just sear the outside of it. Some people cook the meat to death. I think that's a mistake. You want the meat to cook slowly in the pot and soak up all the flavors surrounding it.

After the meat come the beans. Some people cook their beans fresh. I don't. I think canned is just fine.

Everything Is Connected
Important details will always be connected to a main idea or a paragraph topic. Details that have no connection to anything around them will not be important for you to know.

1. **Why should the meat be browned instead of cooked through?**

   A   to avoid burning it

   B   to conserve pans

   C   to save time

   D   to let it soak up flavor

▷ What key word should you read for and underline?

_____

▷ Does the important information supply the answer to the question?

_____

▷ Where is the answer to the question?

_____

• **Identify** the detail needed to answer the question.
• **Find** the first mention of the detail in the text.
• **Closely read** the sentence **before** the mention of the detail.
• **Closely read** the sentence **containing** the detail.
• **Closely read** the sentence **after** the mention of the detail.

Guided Practice

Memo to Employees

To: All employees, 21st floor
From: J. Blenheim, Human Resources
Re: Use of coffee machine

Recent reports to HR indicate that, possibly due to the speed of recent staffing augmentations, employees on the 21st floor are not following prescribed company policy regarding use of the pantry coffee machine. These procedures can be found in section 5(a)iii of the *New Employee's Training Manual.* They are reiterated in this memo for your convenience. Please review the policy and help us all work towards compliance.

1. Coffee machine and all pantry equipment and supplies are for the comfort and convenience of all employees. Be mindful and respectful of needs of fellow employees, and leave a clean, orderly pantry after use.

2. Brown-handled carafes are for regular, caffeinated coffee. Red-handled carafes are for decaffeinated coffee (except at such times as brown-handled carafes are broken or missing, in which case coffee type will be indicated by other markings, such as masking tape). These colors correspond to colors of coffee pouches themselves, i.e., brown for regular, red for decaffeinated.

3. Pouches are stored directly above machine in right-hand cabinet. Each pouch contains coffee for one (1) carafe. Employees are not to use extra pouches or pouch portions to make extra-strong or weak coffee, regardless of their personal predilections. All employees should know what to expect when pouring from a particular carafe.

4. Employees who empty carafes must make fresh pots (see section 5(a)iii, paragraph 2 for official definition of "empty"). To avoid damaging equipment, do not replace empty carafes on hot plate, except at end of day, when machine has been turned off.

5. To make new pot:
   a) Rinse out carafe.
   b) Pull out metal filter holder, remove and dispose of old filter, and place new, paper filter in metal holder.
   c) Open new pouch. Place contents in filter.
   d) Replace carafe on hot plate.
   e) Turn Power button to "Start."

Remember, a courteous and pleasant work environment is a group effort and the result of all employees working together as a team.

1. **Where can employees find the definition of an "empty" pot of coffee?**

   A   Human Resources department

   B   instructions in the 21st Floor pantry

   C   *New Employees Training Manual*

   D   Section 4 of the memo

STEP 1   Scan the questions.

   I should read the passage for the words "empty" or "coffee pot."

STEP 2   Read the passage for the 2Ws.

   Who is it about?   _____

   What does the Who do?   _____

STEP 3   Read each paragraph for its important information.

   The answer to this question is in the paragraph numbered 4.

STEP 4   Return to the questions and answer them.

   _____

Independent Practice

The Good, Gray Poet

Walt Whitman was one of the greatest American poets of the 19th Century. Born on Long Island in 1819, he and his family moved to Brooklyn in 1824, where his father worked, unsuccessfully, as a builder. Whitman attended public school until the age of 10, when he dropped out of school and became a printer's apprentice. As he learned the printing trade, Whitman fell in love with books. He voraciously read everything he could get his hands on. Although his formal education had been severely constricted, Whitman did not let that stop him. He taught himself the works of Dante, Shakespeare, Homer, and the Bible.

▷ **Who** is the paragraph about? _____

▷ **What** does the Who do? _____

Whitman drifted through several occupations during his lifetime. He worked as a writer, a printer, a newspaper editor, a teacher, and even as a hospital aide during the Civil War. Everything he did and everything he saw found its way into his poems, which celebrated democracy and the American people with an exuberant, chaotic spirit unknown to American poetry before him. "I hear America singing," Whitman cried, in one of his poems:

▷ **Who** is the paragraph about? _____

▷ **What** does the Who do? _____

The carpenter singing his as he measures his plank or beam,
The mason singing his as he makes ready for work, or leaves off work,
The boatman singing what belongs to him in his boat, the
    deckhand singing on the steamboat deck,
The shoemaker singing as he sits on his bench, the hatter singing as
    he stands…

▷ **Who** is the paragraph about? _____

▷ **What** does the **Who** do? _____

    Whitman was not concerned with the powerful, the wealthy, and the people living glamorous lives. He lived and moved among ordinary Americans and tried to capture the way they lived.

▷ **Who** is the paragraph about? _____

▷ **What** does the **Who** do? _____

    Some students find Whitman a surprising figure. He does not fit the stereotype many people have of a shy and retiring poet. It is hard to picture him sitting alone, staring moodily at the moon and thinking deep thoughts. Whitman would not have enjoyed that. He loved people and cities and noise. He couldn't get enough of them. It sometimes seems as though he tried to cram the entire world into his poetry:

One's-self I sing, a simple separate person,
Yet utter the word Democratic, the word En-Masse…
Of Life immense in passion, pulse, and power,
Cheerful, for freest action form'd under the laws divine,
The Modern Man I sing.

▷ **Who** is the paragraph about? _____

▷ **What** does the **Who** do? _____

    Whitman's best-known works are his book of poems called *Leaves of Grass* and individual poems such as "O Captain! My Captain!" and "Song of the Open Road."
    Walt Whitman saw many things change in America during his lifetime as his county grew into maturity. In some ways, Whitman can be thought of as having invented American poetry—a poetry that spoke with a truly and uniquely American voice. By the time of his death in 1892, Walt Whitman was well known and much celebrated as the "good, gray poet."

▷ **Who** is the paragraph about? _____

▷ **What** does the **Who** do? _____

Who is the passage about? _____

What does the **Who** do? _____

Main Idea: _____

1. According to the passage, why did Walt Whitman drop out of school?

   A   to write poetry

   B   to work as a hospital aide during the Civil War

   C   to work as a printer's apprentice

   D   to teach himself the classics

   √HINT   Making note of the Who and What of each paragraph will tell you exactly where to find the answer.

2. Which of the following BEST illustrates the difference between Walt Whitman and the common stereotype of poets?

   A   He worked as a hospital aide during the Civil War.

   B   He saw many things change during his lifetime.

   C   He invented a new kind of poetry.

   D   He loved people and cities and noise.

   √HINT   Scanning the passage for key words used in the question will lead you straight to the answer.

3. What kind of people did Whitman prefer to write about?

   A   mailmen and factory workers

   B   kings and queens

   C   generals and presidents

   D   poets and painters

   √HINT   What does reading for the important information tell you?

Test Practice

Read this passage, and answer questions 1–5.

School-Based Management

There have been many efforts at school reform in America. Read this essay and learn about one idea that seeks to restructure the way schools are run.

School-Based Management (SBM) may be the most significant educational reform in decades, and yet no two people agree on what it is, how to achieve it, or even why to do it at all. Defining SBM, therefore, is somewhat problematic. One short definition is "democratic administration." More specifically, SBM is an attempt to transform schools into communities where all the affected parties are involved in making important decisions. No longer the traditional top-down school management structure, SBM requires administrators, teachers, parents, and even students to become connected to the decision-making process.

The reasons for implementing SBM are varied, but the bottom line for most of them is that SBM can enhance student achievement. In an ideal setting, this seems logical. Teachers and parents, who are in direct contact with students on a daily basis, get a say in curricular goals, disciplinary action, and other important decisions. Administrators provide a district-wide perspective that allows for a cohesive learning experience as students proceed through grade levels. The driving theory behind SBM is that everybody can focus on student learning. Of course, not every theory is perfect in reality. Many questions surrounding SBM remain unanswered. How much decision-making power does each party get? Who decides the balance of power? How does SBM function in an emergency situation?

Even with these pertinent questions, SBM is a rapidly growing system of school administration. The most recognizable seeds of this reform appeared approximately 16 years ago when the National Commission on Excellence in Education suggested a restructuring of schools and districts. However, the concept of democratic administration was evident at the beginning of the twentieth century. In 1903, John Dewey wrote, "Until the public school system is organized in such a way that every teacher has some regular and representative way ... [to] register judgment upon matters of educational importance, ... the assertion that the present system is not ... democratic seems to be justified."

The grounds for democracy in education gained strength during the 1960s. A 1966 report from the National Association of Secondary-School Principals stated that the best education of students demands a genuine working partnership of teachers, principals, superintendents, and school boards. This view was maintained, though not officially implemented, throughout the 1970s. The National Institute of Education completed a study in 1977 concluding that schools must integrate teachers and the community into decision-making. The 1980s saw the appearance of SBM itself and the beginnings of policy recommending its implementation into the school structure.

What gave SBM its widest ranging acceptance was the decentralization of power and decision-making in the private sector during the 1990s. As business leaders discovered the competitive and economic advantages of sharing power and knowledge, the idea of decentralization became more widely accepted and popular. Successful companies have found that granting decision-making power to teams or team leaders has given employees a greater stake in the success of the business and has given businesses a deeper and wider pool of creativity upon which to draw.

The sharing of knowledge has been key to American business in the last decade as well, and this knowledge is not limited to facts and details about the company's work. Employees have been encouraged to pursue extensive training while on the job, to deepen and broaden their skills. No longer are employees hired to do one thing and expected to continue doing that one thing forever. Employees at successful businesses are encouraged to take initiative, learn more, and do more—again maximizing the creative potential of the workforce.

Business in America has discovered that innovation—the next big idea that will change everything—may come from any place within the workforce. A business that shuts its ears to the majority of its employees only stands to hurt itself. The old stereotype of big business, with its czar-like executives and its faceless drones at rows of identical desks, is now as outdated in corporate America as the typewriter.

Interestingly, the public sector has proven more resistant to this kind of change. SBM continues to be talked about, argued over, and, in some places, implemented. What role it will play in the future of American schooling remains to be seen.

1. **According to the passage, the BEST reason for implementing SBM is that it can—**

   A   help school boards make decisions.

   B   decrease principal responsibilities.

   C   increase student performance.

   D   raise teacher salaries.

2. **Throughout the second half of the twentieth century, what happened to SBM?**

   A   It disappeared.

   B   It gained strength.

   C   It became undemocratic.

   D   It was implemented in every school.

3. **Which sentence BEST summarizes John Dewey's view of early twentieth century schools?**

   A   The present system is democratic because principals have all the control.

   B   The present system is undemocratic because teachers are not represented.

   C   The present system is democratic because students are represented.

   D   The present system is undemocratic because parents are not involved.

4. **Which organization concluded that the community should be a part of decision making?**

   A   National Association of Secondary-School Principals

   B   National Commission on Excellence in Education

   C   National Institute of Education

   D   School-Based Management Association

5. **What gave the ideas behind SBM wider acceptance in the 1990s?**

   A   the continuing deterioration of public schools

   B   the decentralization of private-sector business

   C   the public endorsement of President Clinton

   D   the sharing of power at the district level

Unit 2 ReKAP

Look back at the strategies in this unit, and review them. Then fill in the spaces below to show what you have learned.

- When reading a passage, the first thing I will do is _____ the

  multiple-choice questions.

- The second thing I will do is read the passage for the _____.

- While reading, I will make note of the _____.

- When I go back to find the answers to the questions, I will find the key words

  and then _____.

READING BETWEEN THE LINES

Thinking KAP

1. What do you think probably happens to the main character of your favorite movie after the story of the movie ends?

   _____

   _____

   _____

   _____

   _____

2. What makes you think this?

   _____

Making Inferences

One of the things that can make reading passages difficult is when the writing *hints* at meaning instead of stating it plainly. When authors do this, they want you to read between the lines, or make **inferences.**

Inferences require guesswork. There can be *better* answers or *most likely* answers, but there cannot be absolute answers. Because of this, inference questions on the CAHSEE are usually phrased with qualifying words or phrases.

When you see words like this, you are probably looking at an inference question:

- why
- think
- seem
- might
- should
- would
- based on
- probably
- most likely
- conclude
- suggest

Inference questions are slightly trickier than the detail-oriented questions we looked at in Unit 2.

- A detail question asks for information *from* the text.
- An inference question asks for information *based on* the text.

▷ Why is it important to know if a question requires an inference instead of a detail?

_____

The Ballpark Strategy

Think of the main idea of a text as a baseball field. In baseball, a hit only counts if it stays "in-bounds," within the limits of the field. Inferences work the same way. All your inferences should fit into the main idea. Even if they go beyond the scope of the story, any inference you make needs to land within the limits of the main idea. If an inference doesn't relate to the main idea of the passage, you know it's out of bounds.

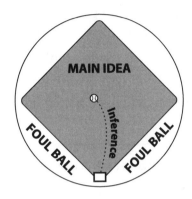

When you make an inference, take a step back and look at the whole ballpark. The trick to making inferences is being able to extend ideas far—but not too far.

Is It Fair to Say?

To check if an inference you are making is in the ballpark, ask yourself:

• Does this inference fit with the tone of the passage?

• Does this inference stay within the bounds of the main idea?

Try It Out!

Read the main idea and use it to answer the inference question.

1. *Main Idea:* **Scientists have spent millions of dollars researching possible cures for some of the world's most common diseases. Which inference is in the ballpark?**

    A   Common diseases will be cured within the next ten years.

    B   Scientists are not going to put any more money into medical research until they find cures for common diseases.

    C   Scientists have done research to inform them about what diseases the largest number of people are suffering from.

    D   There is no research being done on lesser-known diseases.

▷ Why? _____

▷ What if more than one answer choice seems to be in the ballpark?

   • Which is the closest to the main idea? _____

   • Which incorporates the 2Ws? _____

   • Follow the interaction between the Who and the What.

It's In There!
You won't be asked to make an inference that is not supported in the passage. Your inference skills are being tested, not your imagination.

The Connect the Dots Strategy

An inference can be in the right ballpark and still be wrong. How can you make sure that any inference you make is reasonable and justifiable? The best way is to make sure that your inferences are always connected to something in the text.

The way an inference question is worded can tell you a lot about the kinds of connection you should make to the passage. Look at the chart below.

When the Question Says	You Should
What is the tone? What is the mood? What feeling is created?	Underline words that give sensory descriptions: sights, sounds, smells, tastes. How do those descriptions make you feel? How does that feeling connect to the main idea?
What does this event mean? Why did the author include this event? What theme is expressed?	Connect the detail(s) to the main idea. Does it fit within that main idea? Does it support or prove the main idea? Is it a contradiction or a challenge to it? What importance does this event have in the context of the main idea?
Why did the character do something? What was the cause of this event? What was the result of this action?	Connect the detail in question with the its *most immediate* cause or effect. In most cases (but not all cases), the cause or effect will be located close to the detail in question.

Don't Be So Literal
Questions on the CAHSEE may not use exactly these words all the time. Use these words as general guides for finding inference questions.

© 2006 Kaplan, Inc.

English-Language Arts   Unit 3   69

Try It Out!

Read this short passage and answer the question that follows it.

Ivan came in the back door and lingered there, as if he wanted to be able to get out quickly. He kept his eyes on the floor and kicked at the tiles, as though they were loose. His mother narrowed her eyes and tilted her head. "Bad day?" she asked. Ivan shrugged and started making his way across the kitchen, leaning against the walls as if he were afraid to cross the open floor. His mother watched him the whole way, saying nothing. When Ivan reached the doorway on the other side of the kitchen, he bolted down the hall towards his room. When he turned around to shut the door, he found his mother leaning in the doorway, right behind him. "All right," she said, "let's see it." Ivan sighed and handed her the note from his teacher.

How Do You Feel?
Inferences have a lot to do with how the language makes you feel. The *tone* of a story gives you sensory information like the weather, the season, the time of day—things that set the scene and create a mood. The *theme* of the passage is the overarching sense created by the events or ideas being described.

1. **What is MOST LIKELY true about the note from Ivan's teacher?**

    A   It's not very important.

    B   It's about Ivan's participation in the school newspaper.

    C   It's not going to make Ivan's mother happy.

    D   It's going to make Ivan's mother very happy.

▷ What evidence do you have in the passage to make this inference?

_____

2. **Ivan MOST LIKELY lingers by the back door before coming in because—**

    A   he thinks he forgot something at school.

    B   he wants to stay outside and play.

    C   he doesn't want to confront his mother.

    D   he doesn't want to do his homework.

▷ What is the main idea of the passage?

_____

▷ What if you can't find the connection right away?

  • Work backwards until you find it.

  • Ask yourself "Why?" and "How?"

  • Follow the interaction between the Who and What.

Changes

Some questions may focus on the idea of **change**. You will have to do more than identify the main idea; you will have to discuss the *meaning* of that idea, or explain why something happened. Very often, this will involve reaching beyond the stated text. This is where inferences come into play.

In **literary passages**, you might be asked how the events in a story have changed the main character, or what the main character has learned from the events:

1. Why does Tekoa "smile a secret smile" at the end of the story?

In **informational passages**, you might be asked to predict the next step in a scientific process or explain the larger meaning of an important, historical turning point:

2. What will MOST LIKELY happen if acid rain is left unchecked?

3. If the Japanese had not bombed Pearl Harbor in 1941, one possible result might have been—

To help you zero in on the important change or turning point being discussed, go back to the **2Ws** and look at how they affect each other in the passage. Ask yourself these questions:

• How does the **What** affect or change the **Who**?

• How does the **Who** affect or change the **What**?

Usually, there will be a clear answer to *one* of these questions. Most reading passages focus on a single main idea—one process, one change, one turning point. However, you *may* find a more complex passage in which the **Who** and the **What** affect each other. This is why you should always ask yourself *both* questions, even if you can't find an answer for both.

I See A Test In Your Future
Questions about change often require you to make a prediction. As with all inferences, predictions should be based on *evidence*.

Try It Out!

Read this passage and answer the questions that follow.

The Man Who Saved Greece

Solon was one of the Seven Wise Men of Greece. He ruled Athens as the city's chief magistrate in the early years of the 6th century B.C. (594-3 B.C.). Solon is credited with helping to establish the first democracy.

Athens was ruled at that time by nine archons, or magistrates, but the city was really controlled by wealthy aristocrats who owned nearly all of the land. Farmers had fallen deeper and deeper into debt over the years, until the only way to pay their debts was to sell their children, their wives, and even themselves into slavery. The situation for the average farmer was terrible and getting worse, and the people in power, who should have been able to help them, were precisely the people causing their troubles.

In 594 B.C., the situation was bad enough that even the wealthy knew that something had to be done. They agreed to hand over all political power to a single individual, Solon. Solon's mission was to reform the government before a revolution tore the city-state apart, and to make sure that this extreme split between rich and poor didn't happen again.

Soon after taking office, Solon dismissed all outstanding debts. This radical move, seemingly unthinkable today, restored a sense of balance to Athenian society and calmed the fires of rebellion. Then he freed as many Athenians as he could from the slavery they had sold themselves into. He made it illegal to take people into slavery if they defaulted on loans.

Solon then divided Athenian society into four classes based on wealth, and gave each class a role in running the nation. Solon did not believe that ordinary people could rule themselves, but he did believe that they should be consulted on major decisions. He created a popular assembly called the Council of Four Hundred to represent ordinary citizens and advise the leaders of Athens. This council marked the beginning of representative government in Greece.

Which Who?
In questions on major changes, the person or thing being changed should become the **Who** in your 2W statement.

1. **How did the political role of the wealthy aristocrats change after Solon's reign?**

    A   The aristocrats lost most of their influence.
    B   The aristocrats held on to all of their power.
    C   The aristocrats became one voice among many.
    D   The aristocrats became even more influential.

▷ **Who** is the passage about? _____

▷ **What** does the Who do? _____

▷ How does the Who affect or change the What?

_____

▷ How does the What affect or change the Who?

_____

Guided Practice

A Bright Idea

Thomas Edison was born in Milan, Ohio in 1847. As a boy he was very curious and showed a fierce interest in science. He grew up to become a world-famous inventor. In fact, modern life would not be possible without the inventions of Thomas Edison.

On September 4, 1882, a crowd of people gathered at Edison's new Pearl Street power station in New York City. Edison, the "Wizard of Menlo Park," stood ready to flip the main switch that would start up the power station. When the station started working, some 800 electric lamps in 25 nearby office buildings would suddenly light up for the first time.

Edison had long dreamed of this moment. He was sure that people needed the electric light bulb. He would give it to them safely, cheaply. It would make their lives better and make him a rich man. He was confident of that.

But many in the crowd were not so sure. Nothing like this had ever been done before. Edison had struggled for years just to invent the light bulb itself. So had some of the greatest scientists in the world. They all had failed.

By the late 1870s, Edison had fit together some important pieces of the puzzle. He knew that a successful electric lamp should be a closed glass tube, or bulb. All the air should be pumped out of the bulb, creating a vacuum inside it. Also inside would be a thin wire or filament. When electric current passed through the filament, it would become glowing hot and give off light.

The problem was that the current created too much heat. The thin filament wire always melted. Edison tried making filaments out of a hundred different materials, from fine gold thread to human hair. Most of them burned within a few seconds. A few lasted several minutes, none more than a few hours. A filament made of platinum lasted the longest. But platinum is a rare metal and very expensive. One of Edison's men calculated that each light bulb made of platinum would cost nearly one hundred dollars!

Finally, in October, 1879, Edison had an inspiration. He took a simple piece of cotton thread and burned it. The burning covered the thread with a layer of charred carbon. The first bulb with this filament inside it glowed steadily for fifteen hours.

It was one thing to develop a practical light bulb. Now Edison needed to make thousands of such bulbs. He built a factory to do just that. He needed a power station, too, and miles of electrical cable to run current from the power station into those office buildings. Edison worked day and night for almost three years on the project, and so did the hundreds of men he employed.

And now, at last, the moment was at hand. The crowd held its breath. Edison threw the switch. The power plant hummed into action. Then, a louder sound came from out in the streets. It was the sound of people shouting. They stared in amazement at the electric lamps glowing in the windows of those lucky office buildings, and they shouted Thomas Edison's name.

1. **The author of this article is MOST LIKELY—**

   A   suspicious of the benefits of technology.

   B   dismissive of the importance of Edison's work.

   C   interested in the history of technology.

   D   skilled in scientific experimentation.

▷ What is the tone or mood of the passage?

   <u>respectful</u>

Causes and Events
When a question asks you what effect something had, or what an action caused, be sure to look for the most direct connections between events.

▷ Which answer choices do not match this tone?

_____

▷ Which answer choice lies outside the ballpark of the main idea?

_____

2. **What immediate effect did the events of September 4, 1882 probably have on Thomas Edison?**

   A   They gave him great wealth.

   B   They made him respected and admired.

   C   They burdened him with responsibilities.

   D   They made him a world-famous inventor.

▷ What event occurs on September 4?

   <u>Edison gives a public demonstration of the light bulb.</u>

▷ What is the effect of that event?

_____

▷ What change does that effect imply?

_____

Independent Practice

Read the passage below and use the strategies in this unit to answer the questions that follow.

The Mystery of Stonehenge

On Salisbury Plain in England, west of the town of Amesbury, stands a strange and mysterious artifact of the distant past. The stone monoliths known as Stonehenge stand as a silent testimony to an ancient people. Who those people were, and how they constructed this imposing circle of stones, is a mystery that has puzzled scientists for ages.

From a distance, Stonehenge doesn't seem very large, but when you get closer it takes your breath away. The tallest upright stone is 22 feet high, with another 8 feet underground. The massive size of the stones leads people to one of the many unanswered questions of Stonehenge: how did the stones get there?

The original earthwork on the site (called a "henge") was most likely constructed around 5,000 years ago. A thousand years after that, construction began on the first stone circle. The stones weighed up to 4 tons each and may have come from as far away as the Prescelly Mountains in Wales—nearly 240 miles away! Many people have developed theories to explain how these enormous stones could have been moved over such a great distance, but none of these theories has been proven.

The giant stones of the outer ring pose even more of a mystery. The largest weigh as much as 50 tons each. How were such enormous stones moved?

For many years it was thought that Stonehenge had been built by the Druids, an ancient Celtic people described by Julius Caesar and other writers during the time of the Roman occupation of England. Modern scholars have determined, however, that Stonehenge had already been standing for 2,000 years before the Druids.

There are many other legends and theories about the origin of Stonehenge, including a story about giants from Africa and a story involving King Arthur and his magician, Merlin. The truth remains elusive. We know roughly when the structure was built, but we have no clear idea of who built it or why. Was it a temple? A burial site? An ancient calendar? No one is entirely certain.

For all our science and technology—for all the questions of the universe that we've solved—Stonehenge has been, and still remains, a mystery.

1. **Why did the builders of Stonehenge MOST LIKELY bury part of the upright stones?**

    A   to please the gods of the earth

    B   to make them resemble a mountain

    C   to hide the size of the stones

    D   to keep the stones from falling

    ✓**HINT** What makes sense?

2. **What is the BEST evidence that Stonehenge was an important location to its builders?**

    A   Scientists have never figured out how the enormous stones were moved.

    B   Many earlier structures had been built on that site over thousands of years.

    C   Julius Caesar saw Stonehenge during the Roman occupation of England.

    D   The builders decided to use extremely heavy stones.

    ✓**HINT** What information in the article does the question connect to?

3. **This article would probably be MOST useful for someone doing research on—**

    A   architecture.

    B   history.

    C   witchcraft.

    D   stonemasonry.

    ✓**HINT** Which answer choice connects to most of the passage?

4. **What is a central theme of the article?**

    A   Today's logic may be tomorrow's mystery.

    B   Some challenges aren't worth attempting.

    C   Everyone has a story to tell.

    D   People today are smarter than they were in ancient times.

    ✓**HINT** Do all of the answers relate to the main theme?

Test Practice

Read this article and answer questions 1–5.

From Marble to Megabytes

THE HISTORY OF COMPUTERS

> Although the computers we use every day are a 20th-century invention, humans have constructed counting and calculating devices throughout history.

From the moment humans first began to engage in trade, there has been a need for some kind of machine or device to keep track of numbers and perform basic sums. Merchants needed a way to count goods that were being bought, sold, or traded, and also needed to be able to calculate the cost of those goods. The oldest surviving example we have of such a calculating machine is a Babylonian counting board that dates back to the third century BC. This counting board survived through the ages because it was made of marble; most ancient counting devices were made of wood.

The counting board was a simple slab marked with two sets of vertical lines forming ten columns. Each set of columns was crossed by a horizontal line, with symbols carved along the top and bottom. Beads, pebbles, or metal disks were placed on the board and moved from column to column, to indicate numbers of traded goods or amounts of money.

As time went on, this simple device was refined and improved, leading to the development of the abacus. An abacus consisted of a frame that held several rods, with freely sliding beads mounted on each rod. The advantage of the abacus was that the beads or pebbles were not separate from the board itself, making the entire device more portable and useable. Merchants could carry the device with them and slide the beads up or down the rods to keep track of items or perform basic addition and subtraction. When their calculations were finished, they could slide the beads back down to the bottom and begin again.

For many centuries these simple devices served the needs of merchants, shopkeepers, and other tradespeople. As the pace of life sped up, however, people began to look for ways to perform calculations more quickly and efficiently. The kinds of calculations required also became more complicated for business people, and also for scientists and engineers. A machine was needed that could do *more* than what most people could do, and do it faster. The search for such a machine eventually led to the invention of the computer.

A German engineer named Konrad Zuse is generally credited as being the "inventor of the modern computer." At the time, people would have called his invention an "automatic computer" or "mechanical computer." The word *computer* already existed in Zuse's day, but it referred to a person—a human being who computed and calculated things. A computer was not a thing, back then; it was a job title.

In the 1940s, Zuse developed a series of automatic calculators to assist him in his engineering work during World War II, but left Germany when he failed to receive government support for his work. Zuse emigrated to Switzerland and eventually to the United States, where he formed his own company and made several groundbreaking advancements in the field of mechanical computation. He was the first to explore the use of high-capacity memory and the binary system of numbers, both of which are essential elements of the computers we use today. Zuse created the first programming language and, in 1946, the first "computer game," a chess playing program.

At about the same time, a professor named John Atanasoff at Iowa State University, and his graduate student, Clifford Berry, built the first digital computer that used electricity. Among the innovations of the Atanasoff-Berry Computer were the use of vacuum tubes and the separation of memory and computing functions. The Atanasoff-Berry Computer ended up being the size of a desk, weighed 700 pounds, had over 300 vacuum tubes, and a mile of wires. It could perform one operation every 15 seconds. Although this must have seemed miraculous at the time, today's computers can perform 150 billion operations in the same amount of time.

Another early computer, also developed during the years of World War II, was the MARK series, developed at Harvard University by Howard Aiken with the assistance of Grace Hopper. The first MARK computer was a five-ton device, which took up an entire room and was made of almost 760,000 separate pieces. It was controlled by pre-punched paper tape and carried out a variety of mathematical functions. It was used by the US Navy until 1959 for gunnery and ballistic calculations.

In 1946, the ENIAC (Electrical Numerical Integrator And Calculator) was developed by John Mauchly and John Presper Eckert. The ENIAC was another gigantic machine, covering 1800 square feet of floor space and weighing 30 tons. It required so much power to function that it often caused the city of Philadelphia to experience electrical brownouts. The advantage of the ENIAC was its speed. In one second, it could perform 5,000 additions, 357 multiplications, or 38 divisions. However, it took several weeks to reprogram the computer, and the machine constantly required hours of maintenance.

In 1950, Mauchly and Eckert's company was bought by the Remington Rand Corporation, which changed the name of their device to UNIVAC (Universal Automatic Computer). The UNIVAC computer was adopted by the United States government in 1951 for use in tabulating census results. Forty-six UNIVACs were built for government and business use, making Remington Rand the first manufacturer of a commercial computer system. Today, after several mergers and name changes, this company is known as Unisys, and is still a major player in the computer industry.

The general public first became aware of computers in 1952, when the UNIVAC was used to predict the result of the Dwight Eisenhower/Adlai Stevenson presidential race. The computer correctly predicted that Eisenhower would win the race, a fact that many political forecasters in the news media got wrong. UNIVAC quickly became a household name, and the idea of super-intelligent computing machines embedded itself in the American imagination. Science fiction movies predicted both wonderful and terrible consequences of the growth of computers. Some people thought that computers would make life easier for humans in the future; others thought that computers would take over. From HAL in *2001, A Space Odyssey*, to Arnold Schwarzenegger's character in the *Terminator* series, movies have reflected Americans' ambivalent feelings about computers.

The original UNIVAC now sits in the Smithsonian Institute in Washington, DC. If you don't happen to live near that museum, you can see a picture of the UNIVAC by using your own computer to search the Internet.

1. **Which statement BEST reflects the author's main idea?**

   A "Merchants needed a way to count goods that were being bought, sold, or traded, and also needed to be able to calculate the cost of those goods."

   B "Some people thought that computers would make life easier for humans in the future; others thought that computers would take over."

   C "The UNIVAC computer was adopted by the United States government in 1951 for use in tabulating census results."

   D "A machine was needed that could do *more* than what most people could do, and do it faster."

2. **Based on information in the article, what is the MOST LIKELY reason why the oldest counting boards have not survived?**

   A They were destroyed in various wars through the ages.

   B The material from which they were made disintegrated.

   C The abacus rods fell off and the beads were eventually lost.

   D They were dismantled and used to make other things.

3. **The development of computers MOST LIKELY accelerated during the 1940s because of their potential in the field of—**

   A accounting.

   B miniaturization.

   C chess.

   D warfare.

4. **Why were early computers MOST LIKELY taught to play chess?**

   A to show off their calculating speed

   B to prove they were smarter than humans

   C to illustrate their universal appeal

   D to dispel people's fears about computers

5. **This article would MOST LIKELY appear in a—**

   A newspaper.

   B science magazine.

   C social studies textbook.

   D computer manual.

Unit 3 ReKAP

Look back at the strategies in this unit and review them. Then fill in the spaces below to show what you have learned.

• Inferences must be in the same ballpark as the _____.

• If answer choices are *not* in the same ballpark, I can _____.

• Inferences must always _____ to something in the passage.

unit
4
READING LITERARY PASSAGES

Thinking KAP

Write a short story based on the pictures you have seen on the covers of units 1–4.

Literary Passages on the CAHSEE

Now that you have had some practice in making inferences, it is time to take a close look at the type of passage that uses inferences most often: the literary passage.

Some literary texts may be memoirs or autobiographies. Others may be stories or selections from longer literary works. Others may be poems or scenes from plays.

The more you know about the different types of literary passages, the more prepared you will be when it comes time to read them and answer questions.

Play the Percentages
Half of the passages on the CAHSEE will be literary texts, but they can be tricky. Which passages do you think you should you read first on test day?

Try It Out!

▷ What makes a **story** different from an essay?

_____

What are the four major stages of a story?

_____

_____

_____

_____

▷ What do **plays** use to create drama and advance a story?

_____

Where do readers get most of their information in a play?

_____

Focus on Stories

Literary Passages and the 2Ws

You will use the **4-Step Method for Reading Comprehension** to read literary passages, just as you did with informational passages. But literary passages present some particular challenges.

One challenge is that it is often difficult to decide who the main **Who** should be, and what the main **What** is. If you find yourself lost in a sea of Whos and Whats, and you can't tell which is most important, ask yourself these questions.

- Which **Who** changes the most by the end of the story?
- Which **What** has the most profound effect on people in the story?

Literary Passages and Important Information

You already know what makes a detail important in informational passages.

1. _____

2. _____

In literary passages, important information is usually tied to the meaning or lesson of the story, or the effect of the events on the main character. Details that have nothing to do with the "journey" of a character are less important, and usually don't show up on test questions.

Interior Designs
In fictional passages, the most important **What** often happens *inside* a character: the result or effect of the events of the story.

Try It Out!

Read the following passage and then list the main idea and three important details.

Sandy and Sergio had been searching the caves for a whole day. They were exhausted, and Sergio was ready to head home. Finally, though, at the end of the day, they found the celebrated paintings. "They're fantastic," whispered Sandy as she stared at the ancient artworks on the cave wall. Sergio nodded but said nothing. He knew they wouldn't be leaving any time soon.

Sandy aimed her flashlight at an amazingly lifelike representation of a horse. The cave wall was mustard yellow and the lines of the paintings were black. When Sandy got close to them, she noticed that there was a variety of colors—not just black, but ocher, red, rust, and brown. Sandy thought the horse was the most beautiful thing she had ever seen. Sergio couldn't agree with her, though. He had been watching Sandy's face—so happy, so excited by the paintings. He couldn't be annoyed with her anymore. To him, she was the most beautiful thing in the world.

▷ Main Idea: _____

▷ Details: _____

_____

_____

Changes

In literary passages, how characters change is often more important than what they do.

Setting and Mood

The mood or tone of a piece of writing is the overall emotional feeling created by the author.

▷ What things create mood or tone in a movie or on television?

_____

Many things contribute to the mood and tone of a story: concrete things like the setting, the time of day, the season, and the weather; and subtler things like the choice of words (adjectives and adverbs, but also the verbs), and the rhythm and pace of those words.

Try It Out!

Identify the setting of this paragraph, and describe the mood or tone of the writing.

The wind screamed and the rain lashed Burton's face. "We've got to get below!" screamed his first mate.

"You go!" Burton yelled. "Someone's got to keep an eye out for icebergs."

"But Captain—" the boy cried.

"Go!" Burton shouted, pushing the boy towards the hatch.

The first mate ran for the hatch and scooted down, slamming the door closed behind him. The smack of metal on metal sounded eerily final to the old man. He wondered if he'd ever feel the warmth and comfort of below-decks again. But it didn't matter. He wasn't going to lose another ship. Not even if it killed him.

Captain Burton dug his nails into the rail and turned his face into the wind.

▷ What is the setting?

_____

▷ What is the mood or tone?

_____

▷ What elements create this mood or tone?

_____

Characters

In nonfiction passages, authors explain their points directly. In literary passages, however, characters are responsible for communicating the author's ideas and opinions. As a result, understanding who the characters are and how they relate to one another is essential for tackling literary passages.

Understanding characters can be tricky, because you usually aren't told what the characters are like. Instead, you need to look at what the characters say, do, and think, and make conclusions about them based on what happens in the story.

The most important things to figure out about characters are:

• the traits of the main characters in the story
• the relationships between the main characters in the story
• how a character changes over the course of a story

Try It Out!

Look back to the Burton story, and answer the following questions.

1. What adjectives would you use to describe the first mate?

   _____

2. What adjectives would you use to describe the captain?

   _____

3. What can you conclude about their relationship?

   _____

No Fighting
In many literary passages, there is a conflict between two or more characters. When that is the case, expect to be asked about that conflict in the questions that follow.

How Characters Speak

As you just saw, figuring out who characters are by what they say, do, and think is essential for understanding literary passages. Characters appear in literary passages in many ways. Depending on how a character appears, you can determine different things about who that character is. There are four key ways that characters speak in literary passages:

• narration
• dialogue
• dramatic monologue
• soliloquy

Narration

▷ Description: _____

▷ Appears in: _____

Dialogue

▷ Description: _____

▷ Appears in: _____

Dramatic Monologue

▷ Description: _____

▷ Appears in: _____

Soliloquy

▷ Description: _____

▷ Appears in: _____

Get to the Point
Knowing what point of view is being used will help you know whose opinion you're hearing. A character speaking in the first person ("I") is saying what she feels; a narrator speaking in the third person ("she") is saying what she feels *about* a character.

© 2006 Kaplan, Inc.

Focus on Drama

A play doesn't tell a story—it *shows* a story. Events are not described—they *happen*.

▷ How do you know what is physically happening on stage during a dramatic scene?

1. _____

2. _____

In the Mind's Eye

In drama, it's not enough to hear what people say—you also need to pay attention to the *way* people say it. How characters talk can give you important clues about who they are.

Try It Out!

Read the following scene. Try to imagine what is happening on stage.

CARLOS:	Mind if I sit down?
XIOMARA:	Whatever.
(pause)	
CARLOS:	Where you goin'?
XIOMARA:	School.
CARLOS:	Whassamatter? Don't you like them smelly yellow buses?
XIOMARA:	I don't ride them. I live too far out. What about you? Where are you going?
CARLOS:	My grandma's.
XIOMARA:	So…what? You're too good for school?
CARLOS:	I go in the afternoon. I got to take care of my grandma in the morning.
XIOMARA:	Huh.
(pause)	
XIOMARA:	My name's Xiomara.

1. Where does the scene take place?

_____

2. Why is there a pause after Carlos sits down?

_____

3. Why is there a second pause in the dialogue?

_____

4. Why does Xiomara introduce herself at the end?

_____

Guided Practice

from
The Adventures of Tom Sawyer

by MARK TWAIN

Tom appeared on the sidewalk with a bucket of whitewash and a long-handled brush. He surveyed the fence, and all gladness left him and a deep melancholy settled down upon his spirit. Thirty yards of board fence nine feet high. Life to him seemed hollow, and existence but a burden. Sighing, he dipped his brush and passed it along the topmost plank; repeated the operation; did it again; compared the insignificant whitewashed streak with the far-reaching continent of unwhitewashed fence, and sat down on a tree-box discouraged. He began to think of the fun he had planned for this day, and his sorrows multiplied. Soon the boys would come tripping along on all sorts of delicious expeditions, and they would make a world of fun of him for having to work—the very thought of it burnt him like fire. At this dark and hopeless moment an inspiration burst upon him! Nothing less than a great, magnificent inspiration.

He took up his brush and went tranquilly to work. Ben Rogers hove in sight presently—the very boy, of all boys, whose ridicule he had been dreading. Ben's gait was the hop-skip-and-jump—proof enough that his heart was light and his anticipations high. Tom surveyed his last touch with the eye of an artist, then he gave his brush another gentle sweep and surveyed the result, as before. Ben ranged up alongside of him. Tom's mouth watered for the apple Ben was eating, but he stuck to his work. Ben said: "Hello, old chap, you got to work, hey?"

Tom wheeled suddenly and said: "Why, it's you, Ben! I warn't noticing."

"Say—I'm going in a-swimming, I am. Don't you wish you could? But of course you'd druther WORK—wouldn't you? Course you would!"

Tom contemplated the boy a bit, and said: "What do you call work?"

"Why, ain't THAT work?"

Tom resumed his whitewashing, and answered carelessly: "Well, maybe it is, and maybe it ain't. All I know, is, it suits Tom Sawyer."

"Oh come, now, you don't mean to let on that you LIKE it?"

The brush continued to move.

"Like it? Well, I don't see why I oughtn't to like it. Does a boy get a chance to whitewash a fence every day?"

That put the thing in a new light. Ben stopped nibbling his apple. Tom swept his brush daintily back and forth—stepped back to note the effect—added a touch here and there—Ben watching every move and getting more and more interested, more and more absorbed. Presently he said:

"Say, Tom, let ME whitewash a little."

Image Is Everything
Images can communicate powerful feelings and ideas in very few words. Make sure you aren't skipping them or racing through them—they have a lot to tell you.

© 2006 Kaplan, Inc.

1. **Tom convinces Ben to whitewash the fence by—**

    A   refusing to let him do it.

    B   making the work seem like fun.

    C   promising to go swimming with him.

    D   making fun of what Ben is doing.

▷ What is the main idea?

_____

2. **Compared with Tom's feelings in the narration, his words in the dialogue—**

    A   highlight Tom's discouragement at not going swimming.

    B   illustrate his crafty ability to pretend to enjoy the work to get out of it.

    C   describe in realistic terms Tom's excitement at painting the fence.

    D   show Tom's diligence and work ethic.

▷ Where does the dialogue portion of the passage begin?

_____

Independent Practice

from A Doll's House

by HENRIK IBSEN

NORA: Torvald, you have always been kind to me, but I cannot help it. I do not love you any more. That is the reason why I will not stay here any longer.

HELMER: And can you tell me what I have done to forfeit your love?

NORA: It was tonight, when the wonderful thing did not happen.

HELMER: Explain yourself better. I don't understand you.

NORA: I have waited so patiently for eight years; for, goodness knows, I knew very well that wonderful things don't happen every day. Then this horrible misfortune came upon me; and then I felt quite certain that the wonderful thing was going to happen at last. When Krogstad's letter was lying out there, never for a moment did I imagine that you would consent to accept this man's conditions. I was so absolutely certain that you would say to him: Publish the thing to the whole world. And when that was done—

HELMER: Yes, what then?—when I had exposed my wife to shame and disgrace?

NORA: When that was done, I was so absolutely certain, you would come forward and take everything upon yourself, and say: I am the guilty one.

HELMER: Nora—!

NORA: That was the wonderful thing which I hoped for and feared; and it was to prevent that, that I wanted to kill myself.

HELMER: I would gladly work night and day for you, Nora—bear sorrow and want for your sake. But no man would sacrifice his honour for the one he loves.

NORA: It is a thing hundreds of thousands of women have done.

HELMER: Oh, you think and talk like a heedless child.

NORA: Maybe. But you neither think nor talk like a man I could bind myself to. As soon as your fear was over, when the whole thing was past, it was exactly as if nothing at all had happened. Exactly as before, I was your little skylark, your doll. Torvald—it was then it dawned upon me that for eight years I had been living here with a strange man, and had borne him three children. Oh, I can't bear to think of it!

HELMER: An abyss has opened between us—there is no denying it. But, Nora, I have it in me to become a different man.

NORA: Perhaps—if your doll is taken away from you.

HELMER: Nora, not now! Wait until tomorrow.

NORA: (putting on her cloak) I cannot spend the night in a strange man's room. (putting on her hat) Goodbye, Torvald. I won't see the little ones. I know they are in better hands than mine. As I am now, I can be of no use to them.

HELMER: But you are my wife, whatever becomes of you.

NORA: I have heard that when a wife deserts her husband's house, he is legally freed from all obligations towards her. In any case, I set you free. You are not to feel yourself bound in the slightest way, any more than I shall. There must be perfect freedom on both sides. See, here is your ring back. Give me mine.

HELMER: That too?

NORA: That too. That's right. Now it is all over.

HELMER: All over! All over!—Nora, shall you never think of me again?

NORA: I know I shall often think of you, the children, and this house.

HELMER: May I write to you, Nora? At least let me help you if you are in want.

NORA: No. I can receive nothing from a stranger.

HELMER: Nora—can I never be anything more than a stranger to you?

NORA: (taking her bag) Ah, Torvald, the most wonderful thing of all would have to happen. Both you and I would have to be so changed that—Oh, Torvald, I don't believe any longer in wonderful things happening.

HELMER: But I will believe in it. Tell me! So changed that—?

NORA: That our life together would be a real wedlock. Goodbye.

(She goes out through the hall.)

HELMER: (sinks down on a chair at the door and buries his face in his hands) Nora! Nora! (Looks round, and rises.) Empty. She is gone. (A hope flashes across his mind.) The most wonderful thing of all—?

(The sound of a door shutting is heard from below.)

1. **What does Nora want most?**

   A   to leave her husband

   B   to be pampered and taken care of

   C   to be treated like an equal partner

   D   to sacrifice herself for her husband

   ✓**HINT** What a character wants in a scene may not be the same thing as what she does.

2. **Nora's dialogue throughout the scene shows that she is—**

   A   resolved.

   B   furious.

   C   amused.

   D   distressed.

   ✓**HINT** Contrast the tone of Nora's lines to Helmer's.

3. **How does the author build drama?**

   A   by using exclamation points to show the characters' high emotions

   B   by using stage directions to describe Nora's gradual exit

   C   by using dialogue to reveal the characters' points of view

   D   by hiding Nora's intentions from Helmer

   ✓**HINT** Which answer choice makes us ask, "What's going to happen next?"

4. **No stage directions describe Helmer's actions until the very end of the scene. This is done to show his—**

   A   paralysis.

   B   misunderstanding.

   C   unimportance.

   D   arrogance.

   ✓**HINT** What message would the character's motionlessness convey on stage?

Test Practice

Read this passage, and answer questions 1–4.

Zach

When Zach came to pick me up for school he would stand in the doorway and wait for me to see him. He never knocked. Day after day, from sixth grade until we graduated from high school, Zach would come to the kitchen door and…loom. Sometimes my mother would see him before I did, and he never failed to make her jump. His big, round moon of a face framed in the windows of the door was always calm, still, and expressionless. He didn't care how long he had to wait—even in the middle of the winter. He'd just stand there in his parka, waiting to be noticed.

Zach would do anything for effect if he thought the effect was worth getting. We lived too close to our school to be on the bus route, so we walked. Most of the time, this was fine. It was a nice walk, and it gave us time to talk about the important things in life, like whether Godzilla was a better monster than Dracula. Once or twice a year, the trash collectors would pick up anything people left out, no matter how big or strange. Zach loved these days, and he always waded into the piles to find something bizarre. One time, he found an enormous, pink, papier-mâché chipmunk. He immediately adopted it and named it Eddie. All day long, he carried it with him from class to class. This was high school, mind you—not a time when most people carried toys or dolls around with them. But it didn't matter. Zach did what he felt like doing. He danced to the beat of his own music.

One day, when we were seniors, our friend Sam started wearing cool sunglasses to school. He wore them every day, inside and outside. Sam was trying to fit in with other kids at school, and this seemed to be part of his campaign. It was hopeless, but he was our friend so we didn't say anything. Zach couldn't help himself, though. He came to school the next day wearing enormous, clown-sized sunglasses. He looked ridiculous. And when anyone tried to speak to him, he refused to answer. He just smiled.

Sam was annoyed with Zach at first, and as the week wore on, he slowly became enraged. "All right," Sam yelled, "I get the point!" He ripped the sunglasses off, threw them on the ground, and stormed off.

Zach sighed and picked up Sam's sunglasses. "I'll give them back someday," he said. "When we're fifty, maybe."

We packed up our books and headed home. "Do you think Sam understood what you were doing?" I asked him.

Zach shrugged, looked off into the distance, and said, "He will."

Name _____   Date _____

1. **From what point of view is the story "Zach" told?**

   A   first person

   B   third person omniscient

   C   third person limited

   D   second person

2. **What was the first thing Zach did after finding the papier-mâché chipmunk?**

   A   He carried it from class to class.

   B   He named it Eddie.

   C   He found something bizarre.

   D   He walked to school.

3. **One example that Zach "danced to the beat of his own music" is that—**

   A   he walked to school with the author.

   B   he performed in a talent show.

   C   he carried around a papier-mâché chipmunk.

   D   he wore sunglasses.

4. **What is Zach trying to teach Sam?**

   A   not to wear sunglasses inside

   B   not to care what others think

   C   not to look ridiculous

   D   not to come to school

Unit 4 ReKAP

Look back at the strategies in this unit and review them. Then fill in the spaces below to show what you have learned.

- When reading literary passages on the CAHSEE, I will use the _____

   Method for Reading Comprehension.

- When looking for the main idea of literary passages, I will ask myself two

   questions:

   - Which **Who** _____ the most?

   - Which **What** has the most profound _____?

- To understand characters, I will look for their _____ and how they

   _____ to each other.

- To learn more about characters, I will determine when and where they

   _____, and from what _____ the story is told.

- In scenes from plays, I will remember to pay attention to the _____,

   which describe the action, and to the way characters _____, which

   can give me clues about their personality.

unit

5

LITERARY LANGUAGE AND POETRY

Thinking KAP

Choose any **three** of the images below and use them to write a one-stanza poem about love. The poem can be in any style or format you choose—rhyming or non-rhyming, metered or free verse.

_____

_____

_____

_____

_____

_____

_____

_____

Speaking in Pictures

Poetry is a form of literature that requires more inferential reading, or "reading between the lines," than most other forms. Poetry may report facts, as informational passages do, or tell a story, as literary passages do. But poems convey information very differently.

> What makes a poem different from a story or an essay?

_____

Poetic images are word-pictures. A good poetic image can communicate a wide range of ideas and feelings.

Try It Out!

Look at the image below. Then list some words that come to your mind when you think of this image.

_____   _____

_____   _____

_____   _____

_____   _____

_____

Complete Comparisons

A poetic image describes something without having to explain itself. When a writer places two images side by side, these images will seem to be equal or the same. Your feelings about one image will automatically attach themselves to the other. When something is described this way, by making it equal to, or the same as, something else, it is called a **metaphor.**

Try It Out!

If these two images are meant to "equal" each other, what words would you use to describe the person on the left?

_____   _____

_____   _____

_____   _____

▶ What is the shortest, most economical way of describing this person?

_____

The Whole Enchilada
The last line you write on this page will mean different things to different people, because the metaphor does not tell us which aspect of the comparison is most important. The comparison is complete, but it is also open-ended. We are allowed to draw our own conclusions.

Limited Comparisons

Other poetic comparisons are more limited. Only one or some of the attributes of one image are meant to be applied to the other.

Try It Out!

Look at the words between the two images. Then list all of the words that come to your mind when you think of the comparison.

   eats like

_____

_____

▶ What is the name for this kind of comparison?

_____

▶ What other comparisons can you make between people and animals?

_____

_____

_____

Irony

Writers have other tools beyond similes and metaphors that they use to create literary passages. One of the other ways that writers communicate is through irony and its related techniques, subtlety, contradiction, and incongruity.

Irony involves a twist, a contradiction between what is said and what is meant. In stories, irony occurs when words are used to mean the opposite of what they actually say. Ironic statements are often a clue that the author is putting a humorous twist on what he says. In plays, irony usually involves the audience's knowing something that a character doesn't know.

Try It Out!

Read the following paragraph and answer the question below.

Vanity was the beginning and the end of Sir Walter Elliot's character; vanity of person and of situation. He had been remarkably handsome in his youth; and, at fifty-four, was still a very fine man. Few women could think more of their personal appearance than he did; nor could the valet of any newmade lord be more delighted with the place he held in society. He considered the blessing of beauty as inferior only to the blessing of baronetcy; and Sir Walter Elliot, who united these gifts, was the constant object of his warmest respect and devotion.

▶ What could be ironic about this passage?

_____

▶ What words or phrases suggest irony?

_____

So Subtle
Irony is often subtle, so it can be easy to miss. When you read, try to imagine the facial expression the author would have if she were telling you the story herself. Is she trying to contain a smile, that would be irony.

Time and Sequence

In literary passages, authors sometimes play around with the order of events. They may jump forward or backward in time in order to make the story more dramatic, or they may tell the story in an unusual order, such as backwards.

Two of the most common ways that writers play with time are foreshadowing and flashbacks. Writers use foreshadowing to suggest what is going to happen later in the story, while they use flashbacks to jump into the past to explain what is happening in the present.

Try It Out!

Read the following paragraph, and answer the questions that follow.

Yevgraf Ivanovitch Shiryaev, a small farmer, whose father, a parish priest, now deceased, had received a gift of three hundred acres of land from Madame Kuvshinnikov, a general's widow, was standing in a corner before a copper washing-stand, washing his hands. As usual, his face looked anxious and ill-humoured, and his beard was uncombed. "What weather!" he said. "It's not weather, but a curse laid upon us. It's raining again!" He grumbled on, while his family sat waiting at table for him to have finished washing his hands before beginning dinner. Fedosya Semyonovna, his wife, his son Pyotr, a student, his eldest daughter Varvara, and three small boys, had been sitting waiting a long time. The boys—Kolka, Vanka, and Arhipka—grubby, snub-nosed little fellows with chubby faces and tousled hair that wanted cutting, moved their chairs impatiently, while their elders sat without stirring, and apparently did not care whether they ate their dinner or waited.

What time device is being used?

_____

What words or phrases bring you to that conclusion?

_____

What conclusion can you make about the story based on this device?

_____

1. **Which sentence from the passage is the BEST example of foreshadowing?**

   A   As usual, his face looked anxious and ill-humoured, and his beard was uncombed.

   B   "What weather!" he said.

   C   "It's not weather, but a curse laid upon us."

   D   He grumbled on, while his family sat waiting at table for him to have finished washing his hands before beginning dinner.

   What is the purpose of foreshadowing?

   _____

2. **Based on the foreshadowing, what is MOST LIKELY to happen later in this story?**

   A   The children of the widow will return for their land.

   B   The weather will improve, as will Shiryaev's spirits.

   C   A magical spirit will come to help them lift the curse put upon their land.

   D   An argument will ensue between the father and one of the children.

   What can you rule out, based on what you know about foreshadowing?

   _____

Make Sense of It
Poetic language appeals to the five senses. Try to imagine the sights, sounds, tastes, touches, and smells that the author is describing.

Guided Practice

Read this poem and answer the questions on the following page.

answer the questions on the following page.

Line
1   The morning clouds
    Were as white as freshly-washed sheets
    They looked as soft as cotton
    And as playful as kittens

5   Running across the sky
    The cumulus clouds
    Were as big as giants' heads
    The stratus clouds
    Streaked across the sky like feathers

10 Soon, storm clouds appeared
    They raced across the sky like warships
    Cloud after cloud
    Looked ready to explode with rain….

The Main Idea of Poetry
Not every poem will have a main idea the same way that stories or essays do. If you can't find one, look for the main image or feeling.

Step 1 Scan the questions first.

Question 1 is asking _____

Question 2 is asking _____

Step 2 Read for the 2Ws.

Who: _____

What: _____

Step 3 Read each paragraph for the important information.

I underlined _____

_____

STEP **4** **Return to the questions and answer them.**

1. **The author uses similes to describe the morning clouds as—**

   A innocent.

   B dangerous.

   C diminutive.

   D foreboding.

   ▌ What is the topic?

   <u>the morning clouds</u>

   ▌ What images does the poet use to describe or talk about the topic?

   <u>freshly-washed sheets, cotton, kittens, giants' heads</u>

   ▌ What adjectives or feelings do those images communicate?

   _____

2. **Which of the following descriptions of the storm clouds is an example of simile?**

   A soon, storm clouds appeared

   B raced across the sky like warships

   C cloud after cloud

   D looked ready to explode with rain

   ▌ What clue indicates a simile?

   _____

End of the Line
The end of a line of poetry is not necessarily the end of a thought. Use the punctuation provided to help you make sense of the poem.

Independent Practice

Read the following paragraph, and answer the questions that follow.

"The Pale Stranger"

It was a dark and stormy night. The wind howled outside like a lonely wolf. Farmer Jones heard a car screech and tear down a gravel road. "Crazy drivers!" thought the farmer. "Someone could get hurt with a person driving like that." Minutes later there was a soft knock at the door. The farmer muttered to himself about not leaving the outside light on anymore; that way no one would know he was home, and people wouldn't come around bothering him. It was probably a traveling salesman. He opened the door and there stood a pale man, soaked to the skin with rain. The stranger leaned against the doorframe and struggled to say, "Please ...you have to help me." He collapsed to the ground. The farmer quickly dragged the stranger in out of the rain and brought him to the couch. The stranger was breathing but unconscious. The farmer reached for the phone to call the police, when suddenly the electricity went out and the phone line went dead. "Now what do I do?" the farmer thought. It reminded him of another dark, stormy night when someone needed help—the night Maggie had her terrible accident....

1. **What does the use of foreshadowing accomplish in "The Pale Stranger"?**

   A   makes the narrator seem disinterested and bored

   B   shows the reader that the narrator is overly worried

   C   allows the narrator to dismiss the needs of the pale stranger

   D   suggests that the narrator may have reason to be concerned

   HINT Where is the foreshadowing in this paragraph?

2. **Which sentence from the passage is the BEST example of flashback?**

   A   "The farmer reached for the phone to call the police, when suddenly the electricity went out and the phone line went dead."

   B   "Minutes later there was a soft knock at the door."

   C   "It reminded him of another dark, stormy night when someone needed help – the night Maggie had her terrible accident…"

   D   "He opened the door and there stood a pale man, soaked to the skin with rain."

   HINT What function would a flashback serve in this paragraph?

Test Practice

Read this passage and answer questions 1–4.

Convocation

Towards the end of my first week of college, I was dragged away from the comfort of my tiny, airless, cinderblock cell of a dorm room for something called Convocation. I had no idea what I was in for. Nor was I particularly interested. I was having too much fun meeting new friends, staying up till four in the morning, and wandering around the lovely, wooded campus that was my new home. But everyone else seemed to be going, so off I went to the large chapel to see what all the fuss was about.

Convocation turned out to be the official commencement of the school year, and, for us, the official beginning of college. It was supposed to be a very big deal. The entire faculty was present in their academic formal wear—all those gray, dull men and women in their pompous garb. They looked stuffed. They looked like wax dolls.

We filed silently into the pews and sat down, yakking away at each other as if we were in the cafeteria. Up at the podium, someone introduced someone else, who introduced someone else. It was all so much *blah blah blah.*

Then the featured speaker was introduced. He was a professor in the medical school, as well as a published poet. He strode to the podium, tall and proud, and stood before us in his fabulous and regal outfit, his eyes afire and his great beard pointing out at us as if to say, "Pay attention." Miraculously, we shut up. And he began. The poet-doctor spoke to us about education—about the adventure of education. He talked about Christopher Columbus sailing off towards the horizon, certain that there was something beyond it but not really sure. Perhaps there was something. Or perhaps he was going to fall off into the abyss. He didn't know. He set his sights on the limits of his erudition—on the point past which he Just Didn't Know—and he sailed his ship straight towards it. No wonder his crew mutinied! What could be more frightening than sailing straight into your ignorance, with no guarantee that you'll come out on the other end?

This was what education was about, the doctor boomed at us. This was the adventure and the mission that we had undertaken by enrolling in college. Each one of us was to find that Columbus Point—that point past which we no longer knew, but desired to know—and sail ourselves straight for it. It would not be the same point for all of us. We would not all be sailing in the same direction. Nor would we all find the same golden coast awaiting us. There was no telling what any of us might find. Some of us might, in fact, fall off the edge. Beyond the known, there was always risk. Sometimes reward, but always risk.

He rang my head like a bell, and I resonated and echoed with his voice for hours. I stumbled out of the chapel and into the warm, autumn evening, not sure where I was going or what I was doing, but tingling and aware and alive. The other freshmen were snorting derisively and making fun of the whole event. But me—I was heading for the Columbus Point. Already, I felt a million miles away.

1. **Why is it ironic to hear now that Columbus's crew mutinied?**

   A   because we know that he had no idea where he was going

   B   because we know that he went on to discover America

   C   because we know that his crew was unhappy on the voyage

   D   because we know that he had another crew waiting to take their places

2. **Which of the following excerpts from the passage is an example of simile?**

   A   Or perhaps he was going to fall off into the abyss

   B   Nor would we all find the same golden coast awaiting us

   C   It was all so much *blah blah blah*.

   D   He rang my head like a bell, and I resonated and echoed with his voice for hours.

3. **Which of the following sentences from the passage is the BEST example of metaphor?**

   A   Beyond the known, there was always risk.

   B   The other freshmen were snorting derisively and making fun of the whole event.

   C   We would not all be sailing in the same direction.

   D   They looked like wax dolls.

4. **If this passage were part of a longer story, what upcoming events could this section be foreshadowing?**

   A   The author would become a scientist, discovering a cure for a new disease.

   B   The author would not succeed in college and end up in a dissatisfying job.

   C   The author would study the history of Christopher Columbus in her classes.

   D   The author would take up sailing the following summer.

Unit 5 ReKAP

Look back at the strategies in this unit and review them. Then fill in the spaces below to show what you have learned.

- When I am faced with literary language or poetry, I will look for comparisons

  in the form of _____ or _____.

- I will keep an eye out for humor in the form of _____,

  which can be subtle.

- I will pay attention to the way the author uses time, whether through

  suggestion at the future with _____ or explanation from

  the past with _____.

Understanding Vocabulary in Context

Thinking KAP

At the beginning of Unit 5 you wrote a short story. Try to rewrite that story now, without using any words spelled with the letter *E*.

Example: *In Unit 5 you put in writing a short story. Try to do that story again now, without using any words including our writing symbol that follows D.*

_____

_____

_____

_____

_____

_____

_____

_____

Words, Words, Words

Every time you read demanding or difficult texts, you run the risk of coming across words you've never seen before. This is especially true on the CAHSEE, which deliberately includes challenging words to test your ability to make sense of them.

Try It Out!

Define the following words.

feigned　_____

illicit　_____

morbid　_____

If you are unsure of the meanings of these words, don't worry. This unit will supply you with several strategies to answer vocabulary questions on the CAHSEE.

Vocabulary-in-Context

Most of us don't learn words from lists. We figure out the meanings of new words from the **context**. The context of a word is the situation it's placed in—the other words surrounding it. Without any context, new and unfamiliar words can be very difficult to understand. Placed in some kind of context, however, words can be much easier to decode.

Even if you don't know the complete definition, you can usually get close to the meaning of a word in context.

Try It Out!

See if you can use the context to figure out the meanings of these words:

1. Keith **feigned** being sick so he could stay home from school.

   Feigned means: _____

2. The thief kept his **illicit** wealth locked in a closet in the basement.

   Illicit means: _____

3. After watching the sad movie, the teenager was plagued with **morbid** thoughts.

   Morbid means: _____

▷ How does knowing the context help you understand the meaning of the words?

_____

Respect the Environment
Seeing a word in its proper surroundings makes it much easier to figure out the word's meaning.

What You'll See on the CAHSEE

The CAHSEE will almost always give you vocabulary words in context. This will make vocabulary questions much easier to answer. In fact, the vocabulary question will usually repeat the entire sentence in which the tested word occurs.

1. **What does the word *feigned* mean in the following sentence?**

    > By the time Monday rolled around, Jasmine was so afraid of seeing Tanya again that she feigned illness by heating a thermometer on her bedside lamp and coughing pathetically whenever her mother entered her room.

    A   intensified

    B   provoked

    C   craved

    D   pretended

▷ How does this format work to your advantage?

_____

▷ If a passage has one of these vocabulary questions, at what point should you answer it?

_____

Some vocabulary questions may ask you to rewrite a line or phrase from a passage, giving you answer choices that replace the tested word with close synonyms. You will have to choose the one answer that matches the boxed question—or the one answer that does NOT match it.

2. **Which of the following is a correct rewording of the following sentence?**

    > The end of the 20th century saw a great advance in cancer research.

    A   The end of the 20th century has made early payments on cancer research.

    B   The end of the 20th century has seen cancer research become important.

    C   The end of the 20th century has made improvements in cancer research.

    D   The end of the 20th century has made opening approaches to cancer research.

▷ Are these questions easier or harder than the first kind? Why?

_____

Knock Them Down
The best way to get control over a test is to identify the challenges and give yourself a strategy for each one.

Using Context Clues

Certain linking words can provide keys to a vocabulary word's meaning. If you see these linking words in the vicinity of your vocabulary word, there's a good chance that your word is related to another word in the same sentence.

Synonym Clues – Your word may be similar to another word in the sentence:
- and
- so
- completely
- thoroughly

Antonym Clues – Your word may be the opposite of another word in the sentence:
- but
- nevertheless
- despite
- though
- although
- in spite of
- on the other hand
- however

Cause-and-Effect Clues – Your word may have a causal relationship with another word:
- because
- as a result of
- led to

Try It Out!

Circle the Context Clue and predict the meaning of the underlined word in each sentence.

1. Although Scott likes potatoes, his sister Margie **snargles** them.

   _____

2. Because the singer was so popular, the audience **blemmled** when she appeared.

   _____

3. Rusty and unreliable, the old car was badly in need of a **glemgebog**.

   _____

Comma Clues
Commas are used to link concepts. The words on this page will tell you what kind of link to look for.

Using Word Charge

Context Clues and an understanding of the sentence as a whole should tell you whether the tested word has a positive or negative "charge."

Some words have a charge all by themselves.

Disgusting has a negative Word Charge (–).

Lovely has a positive Word Charge (+).

Table may not have any charge at all. It is usually a neutral word (N).

Some words have a charge based on the context of the sentence.

Every time I think of her, my heart is ***filled*** and my soul sings.

Word Charge can help you a great deal on the CAHSEE.

▷ If you know that a mystery word has a positive charge, you can eliminate any answer choices that are _____ or _____.

▷ If you know that the mystery word should have a negative charge, you can eliminate any answer choices that are _____ or _____.

▷ If the mystery word is fairly neutral, you can eliminate any answer choices that have strong _____ or _____ charges.

Try It Out!

See if you can figure out the Word Charge of the following words.

Word	Charge (+, – , or N)
Cantankerous	
Mellifluous	
Pusillanimous	
Placid	

Hiding in Plain Sight
On multiple-choice tests, the correct answer is always right in front of you.

The 3Cs

When you put all of these strategies together, the end result is this:

When you see a word you don't know in a sentence, it's not just you versus it.

There are 3 things that will help you figure out the definition of a word: context, commas, and charge.

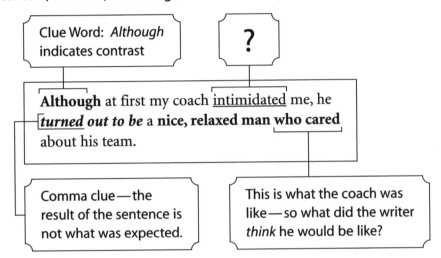

Clue Word: *Although* indicates contrast

?

Although at first my coach intimidated me, he *turned out to be* a nice, relaxed man who cared about his team.

Comma clue—the result of the sentence is not what was expected.

This is what the coach was like—so what did the writer *think* he would be like?

Charge!
Sentences have charges too. So do entire paragraphs. When you finish reading something, you feel a certain way. Use this feeling to help you figure out the charge and meaning of the vocabulary word.

Here's how to put it all together:

3 Tips for Interpreting Vocabulary

- Look for Context Clues in the sentence.
- Use commas to link the word to the rest of the sentence.
- Use Word Charge to predict whether the word is positive, negative, or neutral.

Try It Out!

1. I was just a *fledgling* writer, so I read many books and asked a lot of experts for hints and suggestions.

   Fledgling means _____.

2. Ming can never have too much ketchup; she applies it *liberally* to almost everything she eats.

   Liberally means _____.

Understanding Imagery

Many authors use figurative language to suggest a mood or feeling without defining it in literal, concrete terms. Instead of describing a person or a thing factually, they use words to paint a picture. This kind of writing can be interesting and powerful, but it can also be confusing to readers who aren't paying close attention to what the author is doing.

When an author says, "The sun smiled down on me," does she mean that the sun actually smiled? When an author says, "the room smelled like old socks," is he just giving you a simple fact? No. They are using images to convey a mood, a feeling.

When confronted with imagistic language, your job is to see the picture the author is painting (hear the sounds, smell the smells, and so on). Then ask yourself what feeling the author is trying to communicate with that image.

Worth a Thousand Words
Imagery can say more than regular prose, and with fewer words.

Try It Out!

Read each sentence and decide what feeling each image gives a reader.

1. "The sun smiled down upon me."

    happiness, well-being, everything is right with the world.

    ▷ What image would create the opposite feeling?

    _____

2. "Life is like a roller coaster."

    _____

    ▷ What image would create the opposite feeling?

    _____

3. "The room smelled like old socks."

    _____

    ▷ What image would create the opposite feeling?

    _____

Idiomatic Expressions

Idiomatic expressions are phrases that have different meanings from their literal, word-for-word definitions. They can be very confusing if you have not heard them before. Similarly, figurative language describes people, situations, and feelings by comparing them with things that have a strong sensory or emotional feeling. For example, the words pig, hog, and swine are similar, but they evoke slightly different feelings. Why does an author choose one word instead of a close synonym?

Words in Context
Use Context Clues to help decode any words or phrases you can't figure out.

Try It Out!

Explain what each of the following sentences means.

1. I'm so hungry I could <u>eat a horse</u>.

   The Sentence Means: _____

2. Mom went <u>through the roof</u> when she heard how late it was when I came home.

   The Sentence Means: _____

3. She had the flu and was feeling a little <u>under the weather</u>, but now that it's over, she's <u>in the pink</u>.

   The Sentence Means: _____

4. That <u>mousy</u> girl finally spoke up.

   The Sentence Means: _____

5. Because I was able to choose whomever I wanted for the team, I got the <u>cream of the crop</u>.

   The Sentence Means: _____

6. The snow <u>blanketed</u> the ground.

   The Sentence Means: _____

Guided Practice

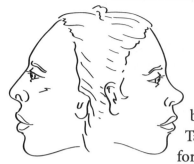

Woman of Two Worlds

Skip It

When you are reading, the overall context is more important than the definition of any individual word. If you hit a foreign word or a challenging word that you don't know, skip it and move on. You can always go back later to work it out.

Did you know that America's first great prima ballerina was a Native American? It's true. Maria Tallchief, born in 1925, has received numerous awards for her lifetime of achievement in dance. In 1953, President Eisenhower gave her a Woman of the Year award, to celebrate her contributions to America. The same year, the State of Oklahoma gave her the Honor Name of Wa-Xthe-Thomba, which means "Woman of Two Worlds," to celebrate her contributions to America *and* to the Native American people.

In more recent years, Maria Tallchief has won a Kennedy Center Honor, has been inducted into the National Women's Hall of Fame, has been awarded an honorary doctorate by the University of Illinois, and was made a member of the International Women's Forum Hall of Fame.

Who is this exceptional woman?

Maria Tallchief was born in Fairfax, Oklahoma, of Scotch, Irish, and Native American descent. She studied with some of the greatest dance teachers of her time, including Bronislava Nijinska, a member of the famous and innovative Diaghilev's Ballet Russe de Monte Carlo and the sister of the legendary dancer Nijinsky.

After high school, Maria danced with the Ballet Russe de Monte Carlo for five years, where she met a young dancer and choreographer named George Balanchine. Maria and George married in 1947, and left the Ballet Russe de Monte Carlo to form a new company, which eventually became the New York City Ballet.

George Balanchine became an influential and famous choreographer, and Maria Tallchief became his prima ballerina. She spent eighteen years with the New York City Ballet, and danced roles in some of Balanchine's most famous pieces, including *Orpheus, The Firebird, Swan Lake*, and *The Nutcracker*. In fact, *The Firebird* was created just for her, to show off her unique talents and abilities.

In 1966, Maria Tallchief retired from dancing to spend more time with her daughter and her second husband. In the 1970s, Maria served as the artistic director of the Lyric Opera Ballet, in Chicago. In 1980, she founded the Chicago City Ballet, where she also served as artistic director.

After a lifetime of achievement, Maria Tallchief sat down in 1997 to write her autobiography. The title sums up her life perfectly: *America's Prima Ballerina*.

1. **What does *descent* mean as used in the following sentence?**

> Maria Tallchief was born in Fairfax, Oklahoma, of Scotch, Irish, and Native American descent.

   A collapse

   B origin

   C fair

   D advance

▷ What are your Context Clues?

born...of...

2. **What does the word *innovative* mean in the following sentence?**

> She spent eighteen years with the New York City Ballet, and danced roles in some of Balanchine's most original and innovative pieces.

   A creative

   B outlandish

   C insipid

   D risky

▷ What Word Charge does *innovative* have?

▷ Which answer choices can you eliminate?

Substitute System
Try reading the sentence to yourself with a synonym in place of the tested word. Make sure the sentence makes sense with your substitute word. Then compare your word with the answer choices. If you find a match, it's probably the correct answer.

Independent Practice

from
A Lecture to Art Students

by OSCAR WILDE

I s it really true that beautiful surroundings are necessary for the artist? I think not; I am sure not. Indeed, to me the most inartistic thing in this age of ours is not the indifference of the public to beautiful things, but the indifference of the artist to the things that are called ugly. For, to the real artist, nothing is beautiful or ugly in itself at all. No object is so ugly that, under certain conditions of light and shade, or proximity to other things, it will not look beautiful; no object is so beautiful that, under certain conditions, it will not look ugly. I believe that in every twenty-four hours what is beautiful looks ugly, and what is ugly looks beautiful, once.

What would you say of a dramatist who would take nobody but virtuous people as characters in his play? Would you not say he was missing half of life? Well, of the young artist who paints nothing but beautiful things, I say he misses one half of the world.

To paint what you see is a good rule in art, but to see what is worth painting is better.

1. **Read this sentence from the speech.**

> Indeed, to me the most inartistic thing in this age of ours is not the indifference of the public to beautiful things, but the indifference of the artist to the things that are called ugly.

What does the phrase *in this age of ours* mean, as used in this sentence?

A   these days

B   in all of our years

C   as old as we are now

D   when we are older

✓HINT Phrases can be tricky. Make sure your choice fits the larger context of the sentence.

2. **What does *virtuous* mean as used in this sentence?**

> What would you say of a dramatist who would take nobody but virtuous people as characters in his play?

A   real

B   interesting

C   uptight

D   moral

✓HINT Go back to the passage and read the entire paragraph, to make sure you understand the context.

3.   **Which of the following is NOT a correct rewording of the following sentence?**

> I believe that in every twenty-four hours what is beautiful looks ugly, and what is ugly looks beautiful, once.

A   Lovely things lose their luster, and homely things gain some, at least once every day.

B   The beauty or ugliness of a thing depends on the values of the person looking at it.

C   There is no such thing as complete and eternal beauty or ugliness.

D   Many external conditions can make something appear uglier or more beautiful.

✓**HINT**   Three of these sentences should mean roughly the same thing. Look for the one sentence that does not fit with the others.

4.   **Read this sentence from the passage.**

> No object is so ugly that, under certain conditions of light and shade, or proximity to other things, it will not look beautiful.

What is the best meaning for *proximity* as it is used in the sentence?

A   relationship

B   substitution

C   condition

D   estimate

✓**HINT**   What other words does *proximity* remind you of? What do those words mean?

Test Practice

Read this excerpt and answer questions 1–5.

Jurgis Underground

by UPTON SINCLAIR

> Upton Sinclair's *The Jungle* was a groundbreaking exposé of working
> conditions in America in the early part of the 20th century. In this excerpt, a
> man named Jurgis discovers the dangers of working under the streets of the city.

The tunnel was a peculiar one for telephone wires; it was about eight feet high, and with a level floor nearly as wide. It had innumerable branches—a perfect spider web beneath the city; Jurgis walked over half a mile with his gang to the place where they were to work. Stranger yet, the tunnel was lighted by electricity, and upon it was laid a double-tracked, narrow-gauge railroad!

It was in a newly opened cut that Jurgis worked, and so he knew that he had an all-winter job. He was so rejoiced that he treated himself to a spree that night, and with the balance of his money he hired himself a place in a tenement room, where he slept upon a big homemade straw mattress along with four other workingmen. This was one dollar a week, and for four more he got his food in a boardinghouse near his work. This would leave him four dollars

extra each week, an unthinkable sum for him. At the outset he had to pay for his digging tools, and also to buy a pair of heavy boots, since his shoes were falling to pieces, and a flannel shirt, since the one he had worn all summer was in shreds. He spent a week meditating whether or not he should also buy an overcoat. There was one belonging to a collar button peddler, who had died in the room next to him, and which the landlady was holding for her rent; in the end, however, Jurgis decided to do without it, as he was to be underground by day and in bed at night.

On an average, the tunneling cost a life a day and several manglings; it was seldom, however, that more than a dozen or two men heard of any one accident. The work was all done by the new boring machinery, with as little blasting as possible; but there would be falling rocks and crushed supports, and premature explosions—and, in addition, all the dangers of railroading. So it was that one night, as Jurgis was on his way out with his gang, an engine and a loaded car dashed round one of the innumerable right-angle branches and struck him upon the shoulder, hurling him against the concrete wall and knocking him senseless.

When he opened his eyes again it was to the clanging of the bell of an ambulance. He was lying in it, covered by a blanket, and it was threading its way slowly through the holiday-shopping crowds. They took him to the county hospital, where a young surgeon set his arm; then he was washed and laid upon a bed in a ward with a score or two more of maimed and mangled men.

Jurgis was ready to leave the hospital at the end of two weeks. This did not mean that his arm was strong and that he was able to go back to work, but simply that he could get along without further attention, and that his place was needed for some one worse off than he. That he was utterly helpless, and had no means of keeping himself alive in the meantime, was something which did not concern the hospital authorities, nor any one else in the city.

As it chanced, he had been hurt on a Monday, and had just paid for his last week's board and his room rent, and spent nearly all the balance of his Saturday's pay. He had less than seventy-five cents in his pockets, and a dollar and a half due him for the day's work he had done before he was hurt. He might possibly have sued the company, and got some damages for his injuries, but he did not know this, and it was not the company's business to tell him.

So Jurgis went out into the streets, in a most dreadful plight. It was bitterly cold, and a heavy snow was falling, beating into his face. He had no overcoat, and no place to go, and two dollars and sixty-five cents in his pocket, with the certainty that he could not earn another cent for months. Words could not paint the terror that came over him as he realized all this. There would be no consideration for him because of his weakness—it was no one's business to help him in such distress, to make the fight the least bit easier for him. He was like a wounded animal in the forest; he was forced to compete with his enemies upon unequal terms.

1. **What does *boring* mean as it is used in this sentence?**

   > The work was all done by the new boring machinery.

   A   uninteresting

   B   gouging

   C   building

   D   smoothing

2. **Which of the following is NOT a rewording of the following sentence?**

   > With the balance of the money he hired himself a place in a tenement room.

   A   With the remainder of his cash, he rented a room for himself.

   B   He found a place to stay and paid for it with his monetary reserves.

   C   He found lodging for himself and paid a fair and reasonable price for it.

   D   He used his leftover money to look for housing.

3. **When the author says of Jurgis that, "He was like a wounded animal in the forest," he is attempting to illustrate Jurgis'—**

   A   aggressiveness.

   B   vulnerability.

   C   illiteracy.

   D   hunger.

4. **Read this sentence from the selection.**

> [The tunnel] had innumerable branches—a perfect spider web beneath the city.

What does *innumerable* mean?

A incomplete

B mystifying

C countless

D finite

5. **What does *balance* mean as it is used in this sentence?**

> As it chanced, he had been hurt on a Monday, and had just paid for his last week's board and his room rent, and spent nearly all the balance of his Saturday's pay.

A stability

B remainder

C equality

D weight

Unit 6 ReKAP

Look back at the strategies in this unit and review them. Then fill in the spaces below to show what you have learned.

- When faced with a word I don't know, I will look for _____ Clues in the larger meaning of the sentence.

- When faced with a word I don't know, I can also look for _____ Clues in the construction of the sentence.

- When faced with a word I don't know, I will try to figure out whether the word has a positive, negative, or neutral _____.

REVISING TEXT

Thinking KAP

Read the text below. Explain in your own words what the author is trying to say.

Me and my boy was going up at the playground after school to hang out and do stuff and stuff. So Ralphie shows me this old Marine Corps ID card from his dad in a little plastic cover. His dad fought and marched and was training, and all like that, but only at a marine camp during the Gulf war in Texas. I went to Texas once, but it was a long time ago. And his dad held onto it. And he meant to give to Ralphie on his 18th birthday. And it was really important for him.

_____

_____

_____

_____

_____

Revision Passages

Some reading passages on the CAHSEE will look different from the others. They will appear to be written on notebook paper. They will be written in a different font and will be double-spaced. In some passages, sentences will be underlined, with numbers underneath them. In others, the sentences themselves will be numbered.

When you see passages like this, you will know that your task has changed. These passages are **revision passages**. You will not get questions about what they *mean*. Instead, you will get questions about how well or poorly they are *written*.

Try It Out!

Read the paragraph from the Thinking KAP exercise again, and underline anything that is poorly or awkwardly written.

Me and my boy was going up at the playground after school to hang out and do stuff and stuff. So Ralphie shows me this old Marine Corps ID card from his dad with a little plastic cover. His dad fought and marched and was training, and all like that, but only at a marine camp during the Gulf war in Texas. I went to Texas once, but it was a long time ago. And his dad held onto it. And he meant to give to Ralphie on his 18th birthday. And it was really important for him.

Say What?

In conversation, you can repeat yourself or reword what you have said. You don't have that luxury in writing. Whatever you say must be clear and correct the first time. After all, you won't be there to fix it when it's being read.

The 4-Step Method for Revision Questions

Revision passages are *not* reading passages.

That's so important, we should say it again. All together now…

Revision passages are *not* reading passages.

You will **not** need to define vocabulary, identify theme or tone, or make inferences. All you will have to do is correct or improve the writing in selected sentences.

These are not writing assignments, either. You will not have to rewrite the passages. All you will have to do is answer multiple-choice questions about writing errors in the passage.

Use this 4-Step Method to save yourself time and focus on what is important.

Why Two Sentences?
In some revision questions, the sentence will not give you enough information all by itself. In most cases, reading one sentence preceding the tested sentence will tell you all you need to know.

The 4-Step Method for Revision Questions

Step 1 Read the first question.

Step 2 Read the sentence preceding the tested sentence, and then read the tested sentence.

Step 3 Predict the correct answer, and find a match among the answer choices.

Step 4 Go to the next question.

▷ What should you do if no answer choices match your prediction?

_____

Try It Out!

Read the following passage and use the 4-Step Method to answer the questions that follow.

> Me and my boy was going up at the playground after school to hang out and do stuff and stuff. <u>So Ralphie shows me this old Marine (1) Corps ID card from his dad with a little plastic cover</u>. His dad fought and marched and was training, and all like that, but only at a marine camp during the Gulf war in Texas. I went to Texas once, but it was a long time ago. And his dad held onto it. And he meant to give to Ralphie on his 18ᵗʰ birthday. And it was really important for him.

STEP **1** Read the first question.

1. **What is the correct way to express the ideas in the sentence labeled 1?**

STEP **2** Read the sentence preceding the tested sentence, and then read the tested sentence.

▷ What is wrong with the underlined sentence?

_____

STEP **3** Predict the correct answer, and find a match among the answer choices.

▷ Prediction: _____

   A So Ralphie shows me from his dad this old Marine Corps ID card with a little plastic cover.

   B So Ralphie shows me this old Marine Corps ID card with a little plastic cover from his dad.

   C So Ralphie shows me this little plastic old cover with a Marine Corps ID card from his dad.

   D Leave as is.

▷ What is the correct answer? _____

STEP **4** Go to the next question.

This exercise has only one question.

What Should You Be Looking For?

The CAHSEE uses revision passages to test your ability to fix the kinds of writing errors that high school students make most often. Here are a few examples.

Boring Writing

The CAHSEE may underline some words and ask you to "describe this more accurately" or "phrase this more precisely." What the test makers are looking for are **active, powerful words** to replace passive, boring ones.

Boring Words:		Better Words:
do	→	accomplish
went	→	journeyed
like	→	adore
thing	→	object
stuff	→	materials
interesting	→	fascinating

When you read the sentences, think about the action or the idea being described. If you were writing the sentence, what words would *you* use to make it more specific and vivid?

▷ What word would be more powerful than "bad" in the following sentence?

> Exhaust fumes from factories make the rain *overly acidic*, which is <u>bad</u> for plant life.

Simplistic Writing

The CAHSEE may ask something like, "What is the BEST way to combine these sentences?" If you see a question like this, you are probably going to be given two or more very simple sentences that can be linked with commas, conjunctions, or semicolons.

▷ Combine these three sentences into one.

> I play the piano. I play the flute. I play the violin.

Awkward Writing

The CAHSEE may ask a general question like "What is the correct way to express the ideas in this sentence?" This tells you that the idea in the tested sentence is being expressed incorrectly or awkwardly. Be on the lookout for the following types of writing errors.

Misplaced Modifiers

Look for sentences that don't make sense when you first read them, and check to make sure that the adjectives, adverbs, and prepositional phrases are modifying the correct things.

▷ Rewrite the sentence to correct the misplaced modifier.

LaWanda ate the cake in the kitchen that her mother made for her birthday.

_____

Sentences That Don't Belong

Some revision questions may ask you to look at *four* sentences (not underlined in the passage, but listed in the four answer choices) and decide which one does not belong in the paragraph from which it came. For each answer choice, you will need to find the sentence, read the sentences surrounding it, and decide whether your sentence fits or wanders off topic. If you have trouble, read the entire paragraph, decide what the 2Ws are, and use that main idea as your guide.

▷ Cross out the sentence that does not belong.

Tekoa has never been outside of Los Angeles, and neither have her three sisters. This week, Tekoa is in Washington, D.C., on a school trip. She has already seen the Lincoln Memorial, Arlington Cemetery, and the Supreme Court building. Arlington was especially meaningful to her. Tekoa has taken many photographs already, and the trip is only half over. Next year, Tekoa wants to visit Chicago. Every night, she writes about her day in her diary, to make sure she remembers every detail.

Vive le Différence

The four answer choices in most revision questions will be very similar. Use your pen or highlighter to identify the subtle differences.

More Awkward Writing

Faulty Parallelism

In longer, more complex sentences, check to make sure that verb forms are all similar.

▷ Rewrite the sentence, correcting the error in parallelism.

  In a triathlon, athletes must bicycle, run, and be swimming.

Some errors in parallelism are trickier. The verb may not be wrong *by itself*; it may just not match the way the same verb (or another verb) is used earlier in the sentence.

▷ Rewrite the sentence, correcting the error in parallelism.

  Olympic athletes train for many hours each day, and even dreaming about their sport is something that can be told to happen sometimes.

Incorrect Prepositions

These errors can be especially tricky for students who are learning English. Be sure you know which prepositions are used in common phrases.

▷ Rewrite the sentence to correct the preposition error.

  Mr. Gresores arrived to the station on the 9:00 train from New Orleans.

Guided Practice

One Sentence at a Time
When answering this type of question, cover one sentence at a time. Do not try to read the whole passage before answering the questions.

> (1) Every October, major league baseball has its championship competition. (2) It is known as the World Series. (3) It is a play-off between the American League and the National League champions. (4) The first team to win four of the seven games in the series wins. (5) Although the name implies that this is a tournament among international teams. (6) It is actually limited to North American teams. (7) In fact, the only team outside the United States that can play in the World Series is the Toronto Blue Jays. (8) Although baseball is also very popular in Latin America and Japan, there is no international competition among professional baseball teams. (9) Only the Little League World Series is a genuine "world series."

STEP 1 Read the first question.

1. **What is the BEST way to combine the sentences labeled 2 and 3?**

STEP 2 Read the sentence preceding the tested sentences, and then read the tested sentences.

▷ What is wrong with sentences 2 and 3?

_____

STEP 3 Predict the correct answer, and find a match among the answer choices.

▷ Prediction: _____

Now turn the page and compare your prediction with the answer choices.

A Known as the World Series, it is a play-off between the American League and the National League champions.

B It is known as the World Series. And it is a play-off between the American League and the National League champions.

C It is known as the World Series, being a play-off between the American League and the National League champions.

D Leave as is.

▷ What is the correct answer? _____

STEP **4** Go to the next question.

2. **What is the BEST way to write sentence 8?**

▷ What is wrong with the sentence?

_____

▷ Prediction: _____

A Baseball is also very popular in Latin America and Japan, there is no international competition among professional baseball teams.

B Very popular in Latin America and Japan, there is no international competition among professional baseball teams.

C Although baseball is also very popular in Latin America and Japan. There is no international competition among professional baseball teams.

D Leave as is.

Beware of "Leave as is"
The last choice in some revision questions says "Leave as is." Do not select this choice unless you are *absolutely* certain that the other three choices do not improve the sentence.

Independent Practice

Thoughts On The Novel

A novel is not an argument or a philosophy. It does not exist to advance a particular theory or idea. A novel is an <u>explore to</u> the world, (1) and its job is to show the world accurately and treat the world fairly. A good novel is like a mirror held up to reality. <u>A novel should be a place of</u> (2) <u>ultimate objectivity, where every character has a right to his own reasons and every character has a right to be understood.</u>

In a good novel, everyone is right. This doesn't mean that every character is good and wise and kind. In fact, the opposite can be true. Villains are usually the most interesting characters. However, in his own mind, every character thinks he is good and wise and kind. Every character has his own reasons for doing things—and thinks those reasons are justifiable.

A novel allows us to view the world the way few of us can in our own lives—with complete understanding and sympathy, without personal malice or prejudice. We are allowed to peer inside the lives of other people and see deeply into their hearts. We don't always agree with what these people do, but we do understand why they do it. It is impossible to hate someone if you truly understand them; <u>the novel is allowing us to overcome our own prejudices and hatreds</u> (3) <u>and see the world with understanding, sympathy, and love.</u>

1. **Which phrase would BEST replace the underlined phrase labeled 1?**

   A   explores around

   B   explore over

   C   exploration of

   D   exploration over

   ✓HINT What part of speech should follow the article "an"?

2. **What is the BEST way to express the ideas in the sentence labeled 2?**

   A   A novel should be a place of ultimate objectivity, where every character has a right to his own reasons and understood.

   B   Every character has a right to his own reasons and to be understood in a novel.

   C   A novel should be place where every character has a right to his own reasons and every character has a right to be understood.

   D   A novel should be a place of ultimate objectivity, where every character has a right to his own reasons and to be understood.

   ✓HINT Is anything in this sentence redundant?

3. **Which change to the underlined clause labeled 3 would make it more consistent with the first clause of the sentence?**

   A   the novel allows us to overcome our own prejudices and hatreds and see the world with understanding, sympathy, and love.

   B   the novel, by allowing us to overcome our own prejudices and hatreds and see the world with understanding, sympathy, and love.

   C   the novel has allowed us to overcome our own prejudices and hatreds and see the world with understanding, sympathy, and love.

   D   Leave as is.

   ✓HINT The semicolon linking the clauses tells us that the verbs should be in the same tense. Which choice matches the first half of the sentence?

4. **Which of the following sentences does NOT fit well in the paragraph in which it is found?**

   A   "A good novel is like a mirror held up to reality." (paragraph 1)

   B   "Villains are usually the most interesting characters." (paragraph 2)

   C   "We are allowed to peer inside the lives of other people and see deeply into their hearts." (paragraph 3)

   D   Leave as is.

   ✓HINT Find the 2Ws for each paragraph and see if the sentence helps to support that main idea.

Test Practice

Read the following passages, and answer the questions that follow.

The Panda

Biologists who classify animal species have tried to categorize the panda according to whether its traits are "homologous" or merely "analogous" to similar traits in other species. Homologous traits are those that species have in common because they have <u>descent by</u> a
(1)
common ancestor. Every species of cat has only four toes on its hind foot. This trait is homologous because every member of the cat family comes from a common feline ancestor. The greater the number of such traits that two species share, the more closely they are related.

<u>For example, a cat and a lion have more homologous traits between</u>
(2)
<u>them than a cat and a human. This shows that cats and lions are more</u>
<u>closely related, biologically, than a cat and a human</u>.

However, what appears to be a homologous trait may only be an analogous trait. An analogous trait is a trait that two species have in common even though they have different ancestors. They just developed in similar ways in response to their environment. The eagle and the butterfly, for example, are not closely related, but they both have wings. Humans don't have wings either.

It is often <u>hard</u> to distinguish homologous traits from analogous ones.
(3)
Analysis of the panda's traits has raised more questions than it has answered. The panda may look like a bear, for example, but its appearance could just be an analogous trait. The panda also has many traits that bears do not possess.

1. **Which phrase would BEST replace the underlined phrase labeled 1?**

    A   descended by

    B   descended from

    C   descent to

    D   Leave as is.

2. **What is the BEST way to combine the underlined sentences labeled 2?**

    A   For example, a cat and a lion have more homologous traits between them than a cat and a human, which shows that cats and lions are more closely related.

    B   For example, a cat and a lion have more homologous traits between them than a cat and a human—so cats and lions are related.

    C   For example, a cat and a lion have more homologous traits between them than a cat and a human, because a cat and a lion are more close than a cat and a human.

    D   Leave as is.

3. **In order to achieve more precise meaning, the underlined word labeled 3 should be changed to—**

    A   confusing.

    B   unpleasant.

    C   difficult.

    D   impossible.

4. **Which of the following sentences does NOT fit well in the paragraph in which it is found?**

    A   "Humans don't have wings either." (second paragraph)

    B   "The panda also has many traits that bears do not possess." (fourth paragraph)

    C   "Every species of cat has only four toes on its hind foot." (second paragraph)

    D   "They just developed in similar ways in response to their environment." (third paragraph)

Editorial from the Sludgeville Bacon

(1) As we all know, a recent plague of shoplifting in Sludgeville has led local storeowners to install security cameras and hire extra security guards to monitor their stores. (2) The storeowners claim they have no choice but to pursue this course. (3) These guards have been given explicit instructions to follow and harass teenagers. (4) They are told to do this any time teenagers enter a store. (5) We at the Sludgeville Bacon are outraged, insulted, and we think it's a scandal that people say local teenagers are responsible for this wave of shoplifting. (6) No proof has been offered by the police or the storeowners that this is true, and the few arrests that have been made have all been of adults. (7) Sludgeville's teenagers are being prosecuted just because they are teenagers, and this is wrong.

(8) Parents and teachers reading this editorial may argue that we are overreacting, that this just a minor inconvenience. (9) However, the fact that we are teenagers doesn't mean that we have no rights. (10) We have the same right to privacy in our town as any other people. (11) We have the right to walk down the street with our friends, and we have the right to walk in and out of shops without being followed and bothered. (12) If we are not breaking laws or bothering other people, we have the right to be left alone, like any other American.

5. **What is the BEST way to combine the ideas in the sentences labeled (3) and (4)?**

   A   These guards have been given explicit instructions to follow and harass them in stores.

   B   These guards are told according to explicit instructions on following and harassing to do so to teenagers in stores.

   C   These guards have been given explicit instructions to follow and harass teenagers whenever teenagers enter a store.

   D   Leave as is.

6. **Which change to the underlined portion of the sentence labeled (5) would make it more consistent with the first part?**

   A   and scandalized that people say local teenagers are responsible for this wave of shoplifting.

   B   and we are scandalized that people say local teenagers are responsible for this wave of shoplifting.

   C   and people should not say that local teenagers are responsible for this wave of shoplifting.

   D   Leave as is.

7. **To more accurately describe the harassment of teenagers by security guards, the word "wrong" in the sentence labeled (7) should be changed to—**

   A   unjust.

   B   mistaken.

   C   confusing.

   D   faulty.

8. **What is the correct way to express the ideas in the sentence labeled (10)?**

   A   We have the same right in our town to privacy as any other people.

   B   In our town. We have the same right to privacy as any other people.

   C   As any other people in our town, we also have rights to privacy.

   D   We have the same right to privacy as any other people in our town.

Unit 7 ReKAP

Look back at the strategies in this unit, and review them. Then fill in the spaces below to show what you have learned.

• The one thing I should *not* do when faced with a revision passage is

   _____.

• The first thing I *should* do is read the _____.

• When I go to the text, I should read two sentences:

   the one _____ and

   the one _____.

• Before I look at the answer choices, I should _____.

unit

8

ANSWERING GRAMMAR
QUESTIONS

Thinking KAP

Proofread and correct the following paragraph. You can make corrections on the text itself or recopy the paragraph correctly in the space below.

There are less advantages to a system of absolute power one advantage is that a absolute monarch is able to carrying out the functions of Government more efficient there is no interference or time wastes when a decision have to be made however governments purpose is not to be efficient it is to reflect the will of the people which is an idea from the period known as the enlightenment there is many disadvantages to absolute control by the one or the few it is a system of governments that is ultimately corrupt and oppressive.

_____

_____

_____

_____

_____

_____

_____

Writing Conventions

In Unit 7, we looked at revision questions, the CAHSEE tasks that test your knowledge of writing strategies and writing conventions. There are other multiple-choice questions on the CAHSEE that test your writing skills. They focus on basic grammar and usage and are not connected to reading passages.

Try It Out!

How many of these writing rules do you remember?

1. Capital letters are always used in _____.
   This question has several answers. Pick one!

2. Commas should never be used to separate two _____.

3. Place a question mark *inside* quotation marks only when _____.

4. The verb in a sentence must always agree with its _____.

5. Titles of books should always be _____.
   This question has two answers. Write both of them!

You will see two types of grammar and usage questions on the CAHSEE: underlined questions and fill-in-the-blank questions. In this unit, we will look at both of them.

Isolation Tank

Grammar rules are hard to remember all by themselves, but don't worry: the CAHSEE only tests grammar rules "in action," as parts of sentences.

Underlined Questions

Some of the grammar and usage questions on the CAHSEE will look similar to the revision questions you saw in Unit 7. However, these questions will have no reading passages attached, and most will focus more on grammar than on the quality and style of the writing.

Underlined questions focus on one piece of a sentence and offer several possible alternatives.

1. The film *Jaws* <u>was releasing in the 1970s.</u>

    A releasing in the 1970s.

    B released in the 1970s.

    C was released in the 1970s.

    D Leave as is.

Taking a step-by-step approach will help you unlock even the most confusing questions and keep you from overthinking them.

Leave As Isn't
Beware of choice (D) in these questions. Most grammar questions on the CAHSEE *will* contain an error. Choose "Leave as is" only if you are *absolutely* certain there is no error.

The 3-Step Method for Underlined Questions

Step **1** Identify the error.

Step **2** Make a prediction.

Step **3** Plug in the answer choices.

A Closer Look at the Method

Identifying the Error

When you look at the underlined part of the sentence, see if you can identify what is wrong with it. You don't need to know how to *fix* it at this stage. Just figure out why the sentence is incorrect as written.

▷ Identify the error in this sentence:

Javier was <u>hungry; although he had made</u> himself a sandwich.

_____

If you can't find an error in the underlined part of the sentence, there may not be one. The "leave as is" choice might be correct. But always be suspicious of that choice. It is not correct very often.

Predicting

Predicting can help you avoid some of the more distracting, tricky answer choices. You can make predictions even if you are not exactly sure how the error should be fixed. Predict the correct answer if you know it—but if you don't know it, just predict which part of the sentence will be fixed in the correct answer. Some answer choices may focus on a different aspect of the sentence or correct something that isn't wrong. Cross them out!

▷ Predict which part of this sentence will be fixed in the correct answer choice:

Javier was <u>hungry; although he had made</u> himself a sandwich.

_____

▷ Based on your prediction, which of these choices can safely be eliminated?

    A   Javier was hungry, although he had made himself a sandwich.
    B   Javier was hungry; even though he had made himself a sandwich.
    C   Javier was hungry; although he was making himself a sandwich.

Plugging in the Answer Choices

In many cases, you will not need Step 3. If you can predict the correct answer and find an answer choice that matches, you are finished.

If you can predict the part of the sentence that should be fixed, and only one answer choice addresses that part, you are finished.

Sometimes, though, your prediction will help you eliminate only one or two choices. You will not have the correct answer yet. When this happens, move on to Step 3.

Take the remaining answer choices, and plug them back into the sentence to see if they sound correct. Read them quietly aloud to yourself. Use your ears to see which choice sounds best.

Get Close
If you can eliminate even one answer choice, you will greatly increase your chances of finding the correct answer.

Try It Out!

Use all three steps of the method to attack this question.

1. **The film *Jaws* <u>was releasing in the 1970s.</u>**

    A   releasing in the 1970s.

    B   released in the 1970s.

    C   was released in the 1970s.

    D   Leave as is.

STEP 1 Identify the error.

▷ What is wrong with the sentence?

_____

▷ Which answer choice can you eliminate now? _____

STEP2 Make a prediction.

▷ What part of the sentence needs correcting?

_____

▷ Which answer choice can you eliminate now? _____

STEP 3 Plug in the answer choices.

▷ Which answer choices sound wrong? _____

▷ What is the correct answer? _____

Fill-in-the-Blank Questions

Fill-in-the-blank questions look similar to underlined questions, but instead of underlined words, you will see a blank line to be filled in.

2. **Which of the four Vlahakis brothers is the _____?**

    A smarter

    B smartest

    C more smart

    D most smart

Plug It In

Predicting does not work very well in fill-in-the-blank questions because it is difficult to know what to predict unless you look at the answer choices first.

Because of this, it is best to jump straight to Step 3 ("Plug in the answer choices").

Try It Out!

Which sentence sounds "right" to your ears?

1. Which of the four Vlahakis brothers is the **smarter?**

2. Which of the four Vlahakis brothers is the **smartest?**

3. Which of the four Vlahakis brothers is the **more smart?**

4. Which of the four Vlahakis brothers is the **most smart?**

▷ What would the correct answer be if there were only two brothers?

_____

Classic Errors

The CAHSEE will not ask you about every grammar and usage rule in the English language. The test makers tend to focus on the most common errors, the kinds of errors most high school students tend to make in their writing assignments. Here are a few classic errors.

Agreement

Subjects must agree with their verbs. A singular subject needs a singular verb; a plural subject needs a plural verb. Nouns linked by *and* require a plural verb; Nouns linked by *or* require a singular verb.

▷ Sharon and Jamie (go / goes / going) to the store.

▷ Either Martin or Russ (has / have / having) my notes from class.

Pronouns must agree with their antecedents (the words to which they refer). Nouns linked by *and* require a plural pronoun; Nouns linked by *or* require a singular pronoun.

▷ Nicole and Tito said that _____ could not attend tomorrow's meeting.

▷ Either Taisha or Maria left _____ books in the classroom.

Capitalization

Capitalize directions only when they are used as nouns (names of places). Use lowercase if they are adverbs (describing which way to go).

▷ To get to my house, drive (West / west) on Route 9.

▷ She has an accent because she grew up in the (South / south).

Capitalize job titles *only* when they are used as part of someone's name.

▷ George Washington was the first (president / President) of the United States.

▷ My city has a statue of (president / President) Washington.

Punctuation

Commas have many functions. On the CAHSEE, use common sense to check how commas are placed in answer choices. Are they separating things that *logically* require separation?

▷ Which sentence is punctuated correctly?

1. I like brown rice, but I really love fried rice.

2. I like brown rice but, I really love fried rice.

Question marks go *inside* quotation marks when the quoted words themselves are a question. They go *outside* the quotation marks when the entire sentence is a question.

▷ Which sentence is punctuated correctly?

1. Why did she say "Boo?"

2. Why did she say "Boo"?

Sentence Fragments

Some sentences that have subjects and verbs can still be fragments if they begin with conditional phrases like *because, except,* and *although.* These words create a seesaw sentence, with a comma as the pivot. ("Because I studied, I got good grades.") If both halves of the seesaw are not in the sentence, you probably have a fragment. ("Because I studied.")

▷ Which group of sentences contains a fragment?

1. I like school well enough. I guess.

2. I'll go with you to the movies. Unless I have homework.

Run-On Sentences

Independent clauses (grammatically complete ideas that can stand alone as sentences) cannot be linked with a comma *unless* there is also a conjunction (*and, if, but,* etc.) If there is no conjunction, the clauses must be separated by a period or a semicolon. Use a semicolon only if the ideas in the clauses are closely related.

▷ Which sentences are punctuated correctly?

1. Robinson Crusoe was stranded on an island, he learned to survive in the woods.

2. The tiger rushed towards my face; tigers are fascinating animals.

Make a Top Ten List
Since the CAHSEE targets the kinds of grammar errors that most students make, look back at old papers you've written, and brush up on the areas where you've tended to make mistakes.

Superlatives

When two things are compared, one of them can be *bigger*, *better*, or *smarter*, but it cannot be *biggest*, *best*, or *smartest*. Use *–er* when comparing two things; use *–est* when comparing three or more.

When you have a word of three or more syllables, use *more* or *most* instead of the *–er* or *–est* endings.

▷ The poetry of Rita Dove is the _____ literature I've read this year.

(interestingest / most interesting / more interestinger / more interesting)

Passive Voice

Passive voice refers to writing that puts the verbs in front of the subjects ("was eaten by me") instead of the traditional, more active construction ("I ate"). Whenever you see an underlined verb followed by the word "by" and the subject, be ready to eliminate answer choices that don't reverse the passive construction.

▷ How would you rewrite this sentence?

When the tests were collected by the teacher, I breathed a sigh of relief.

_____

Citation

When book titles are mentioned in a text, they should be capitalized and underlined. Shorter works, like magazine articles and short stories, should be placed in quotes. Nothing should *ever* be placed in quotes *and* underlined. If you see that in an answer choice, eliminate it.

When quoting from a text, make sure the *entire* quotation appears between quotation marks. If the quotation is broken up by things like "he said," or "according to the author," make sure that these comments lie *outside* the quotation.

▷ Insert quotation marks where they belong in this sentence.

Watch out for misplaced modifiers, he said sternly. They show up in this section of the test, as well as in the revision questions. Then he told me to read the sidebar.

Misplaced Alert
Beware of adjectives and prepositions that are placed far away from the things they describe. The further apart they are, the greater the chance that they have been misplaced.

Guided Practice

Don't Limit Yourself
Errors that we discussed in Unit 7 may also be tested in this section of the CAHSEE.

1. When I <u>turned sixteen my father</u> gave me his old watch.

    A   turned sixteen, my father

    B   turned, sixteen my father

    C   turned sixteen my father,

    D   Leave as is.

STEP **1**   Identify the error.

▷ What is wrong with the sentence?

   <u>It is missing a comma.</u>

▷ Which answer choice can you eliminate now? _____

STEP **2**   Make a prediction.

▷ What part of the sentence needs correcting?

   _____

▷ Which answer choice can you eliminate now? _____

STEP **3**   Plug in the answer choices.

▷ Which answer choices sound wrong? _____

▷ What is the correct answer? _____

2. Helen of Troy was the _____ woman in the world.

    A   beautifulest

    B   more beautiful

    C   most beautiful

    D   most beautified

STEP **3**   Plug in the answer choices.

▷ Which answer choices sound wrong? _____

▷ What is the correct answer? _____

3. Some animals _____ their color to blend into their surroundings.

    A change

    B changes

    C is changing

    D has changed

STEP 3 Plug in the answer choices.

▷ Which answer choices sound wrong? _____

▷ What is the correct answer? _____

4. Stravinsky's music caused a riot at <u>first and people</u> threw tomatoes at the orchestra.

    A first: people

    B first; people

    C first; People

    D Leave as is.

STEP 1 Identify the error.

▷ What is wrong with the sentence?

_____

▷ Which answer choice can you eliminate now? _____

STEP2 Make a prediction.

▷ What part of the sentence needs correcting?

    <u>The clauses need to be separated.</u> _____

▷ Which answer choice can you eliminate now? _____

STEP 3 Plug in the answer choices.

▷ Which answer choices sound wrong? _____

▷ What is the correct answer? _____

And?
When *and* links two objects or verbs, it usually does not need a comma (unless it comes at the end of a list). When *and* links two independent clauses, it must have a comma.

Stumped?

You may be able to find clues in the sentences to help you find the correct answer. Question 5 on this page has a clue to help you find the correct verb tense. What is it?

5. Today, people around the world _____ instantaneously through email and the Internet.

    A communicate

    B communicates

    C communicated

    D is communicated

STEP **3** Plug in the answer choices.

▶ Which answer choices sound wrong? _____

▶ What is the correct answer? _____

Independent Practice

1. New evidence suggests that El Niño
    _____ the world's weather for
    more than 15,000 years.

    A has been shaping

    B had been shaping

    C have been shaping

    D is shaping

    HINT Eliminate choices that do
    not agree with the subject in
    number. Then focus on the
    verb tense.

2. As she entered the office, Rachelle said,
    "Hello, is anyone <u>there?</u>

    A there

    B there"?

    C there?"

    D Leave as is.

    HINT Which two choices can you
    eliminate right away?

3   Neither Glen nor Glenda _____
    much about Astronomy.

    A know

    B knows

    C are knowing

    D is knowing

    HINT Is the subject singular
    or plural?

4   The Mississippi River, one of the longest in
    the United States, flows <u>South from its</u>
    origin.

    A south from it's

    B South from it's

    C south from its

    D Leave as is.

    HINT Identify the error first, before
    looking at the answer choices.

5. Did you know that <u>doctor Liu is going</u> to receive an award next week?

   A   doctor Liu, is going

   B   Doctor liu is going

   C   Doctor Liu is going

   D   Leave as is.

   ✓**HINT** What do you do with titles used as part of people's names?

6. <u>Picasso, my favorite artist used</u> many different shapes in his paintings.

   A   Picasso my favorite artist used

   B   Picasso, my favorite artist, used

   C   Picasso, my favorite, artist used

   D   Leave as is.

   ✓**HINT** Which use of commas makes logical sense?

7. The Olympic Games are the _____ athletic contest in the world.

   A   old

   B   older

   C   oldest

   D   most old

   ✓**HINT** How many things are being compared?

8. When hiking, be sure to take along some <u>insect repellent, mosquito netting, water bottles, and a hat.</u>

   A   insect repellent, mosquito netting, water bottles and a hat.

   B   insect repellent, mosquito netting, water bottles and, a hat.

   C   insect repellent, mosquito netting water bottles, and a hat.

   D   Leave as is.

   ✓**HINT** Don't skip the first step! It can save you a lot of time.

Test Practice

Choose the answer that is the most effective substitute for each underlined part of the sentence. If no substitution is necessary, choose "Leave as is."

1. Shania groaned and said, <u>"Do I really have to go there"?</u>

   A "do I really have to go there"?

   B "Do I really have to go their"?

   C "Do I really have to go there?"

   D Leave as is.

2. My aunt lives on the <u>West Coast, where its</u> sunny most of the time.

   A West Coast where its

   B West Coast, where it's

   C west coast, where its

   D Leave as is.

3. In the novel <u>Candide, by Voltaire,</u> Candide is a simple and trusting soul.

   A Candide by Voltaire

   B "Candide," by Voltaire,

   C <u>Candide</u>, by Voltaire,

   D Leave as is.

4. When the party was over, the DJ packed up her <u>speakers, records, and took her extra party favors.</u>

   A speakers, records, and extra party favors.

   B speakers records and took her extra party favors.

   C speakers, records, and takes her extra party favors.

   D Leave as is.

5. <u>Because the virus is so contagious, flu outbreaks</u> tend to turn into epidemics.

   A Because the virus is so contagious flu outbreaks

   B Because the virus is so contagious; flu outbreaks

   C Because the virus is so contagious. Flu outbreaks

   D Leave as is.

6. <u>Standing in silence Kirsten</u> dreamed of the day when she would be the one people were applauding.

   A Standing, in silence Kirsten

   B Standing, in silence, Kirsten

   C Standing in silence, Kirsten

   D Leave as is.

7. On July 8, 1776, <u>The Declaration was read to the crowd by the mayor.</u>

   A the declaration was read to the crowd by the Mayor.

   B the mayor read the declaration to the crowd.

   C to the crowd, the mayor read the Declaration.

   D Leave as is.

8. "Are you nervous? I <u>would be," said Julia. "someday</u> I'll be more brave."

   A would be," said Julia. "Someday

   B would be, said Julia." Someday

   C would be said Julia. Someday

   D Leave as is.

9. The letters U.S., which stood for United States, _____ on top of canned rations.

   A   will stamp

   B   are stamping

   C   has been stamped

   D   were stamped

10. No matter what we say to him, that boy still thinks a lot of _____.

    A   himself

    B   itself

    C   ourselves

    D   themselves

11. Endangered animals are those whose populations have been reduced almost to the point of _____.

    A   extinct

    B   extinction

    C   most extinct

    D   extincted

12. Several factors _____ to the problem of acid rain.

    A   contributes

    B   is contributing

    C   has contributed

    D   contribute

13. The coach paced back and forth on the _____ knew that this was the deciding moment of the game.

    A   sidelines he

    B   sidelines, he

    C   sidelines; he

    D   sidelines and he

14. This page contains information that students _____ before.

    A   have seen

    B   has seen

    C   seen

    D   will see

15. There were other ancient societies that _____ the views of most civilizations during that period.

    A   were not reflective

    B   did not reflect

    C   had not reflected

    D   were reflecting not

16. In Williams' brief poem, _____, a simple image conveys so much.

    A   The Red Wheelbarrow

    B   The "Red Wheelbarrow"

    C   "The Red Wheelbarrow"

    D   "The Red Wheelbarrow"

Unit 8 ReKAP

Look back at the strategies in this unit and review them. Then fill in the spaces below to show what you have learned.

- In underlined questions, the first thing I should do is _____

  _____.

- Before I look at the answer choices, I should try to _____ the

  correct answer or at least the part of the sentence that will be fixed in the

  correct answer choice.

- I should use my prediction to _____ incorrect answer choices.

- If I still don't have the answer, I should _____ the answer

  choices back into the sentence to see what sounds right.

- On fill-in-the-blank questions, I should _____.

WRITING AN ESSAY

Thinking KAP

Describe your room at home. Provide as much detail as you think is necessary for someone to be able to picture your room accurately.

_____

_____

_____

_____

_____

_____

_____

_____

_____

_____

_____

_____

_____

_____

_____

Exposing the Essay

You will write one essay as part of the CAHSEE. The essay will fall into one of two general categories: writing in response to a question or "prompt," or writing in response to a reading passage. We will deal with the second type in the next unit. Today, we will look at the response to a prompt.

Essays in response to a prompt can be any of five different types:

Biographical Narratives

▷ What is the goal of a biographical narrative?

_____

Analytical (Expository) Essays and Reports

▷ What is the goal of an analytical essay?

_____

Persuasive Essays

▷ What is the goal of a persuasive essay?

_____

Business Letters

▷ What is the goal of a business letter?

_____

Technical Documents

▷ What is the goal of a technical document?

_____

Why Bother?
Essays are formal pieces of writing, constructed according to a fairly tight formula. They make it easier for writers to communicate ideas and opinions in a linear, logical way.

Try It Out!

Decide which type of essay each sentence would probably come from and mark an (N) for narrative, (A) for analytical, (P) for persuasive, (B) for business letter, or (T) for technical documents.

_____ There are three simple steps to fixing a flat tire.

_____ Television shows must be censored to protect young people.

_____ Bilingualism has been the subject of much discussion in the public domain.

_____ Take the third left after the traffic light, and stay right at the fork in the road.

_____ Marian Anderson, the renowned singer, faced racial discrimination throughout her life.

_____ The United States must be the world's policeman.

_____ Renata Swanglehorn stood on the balcony and surveyed the street.

_____ If you have any further questions, feel free to contact me at your convenience.

_____ As gas prices rise, new cars on the market tend to be more fuel efficient.

_____ Thank you for taking the time to meet with me yesterday.

What is "Good"?

What are CAHSEE essay scorers looking for in your writing? What makes an essay "good"?

Essay readers will look at six aspects of your writing and then assign your essay a score between 1 and 4.

Completeness

▷ How can you tell if your essay is complete?

_____

Organization

▷ How are essays supposed to be organized?

_____

Jacket and Tie Required
An essay is a formal, tightly organized form of writing. Sloppy construction, conversational language, or a casual tone can work against you and lower your score.

Support

▷ How can you tell if an essay has enough support?

_____

Language

▷ What are some signs of mature and sophisticated use of language?

_____

Audience

▷ Why does the audience for an essay matter?

_____

Conventions

▷ What are language conventions?

_____

These criteria will all factor into your score, which will range from 1 to 4.

A 4-point essay will be complete, well organized, and well supported, with a clear sense of audience and a mature command of language use and conventions.

A 1-point essay will be incomplete, poorly organized, and lacking in supporting detail, with no sense of audience, a limited vocabulary, and serious errors in language conventions.

So…what can you do to increase your chances of scoring well on the essay?

The 4-Step Method for Writing Essays

The best way to ensure success in essay writing is to approach the task in a systematic, step-by-step manner, so that you never have to wonder what to do next.

Kaplan's 4-Step Method will help you plan and outline a well-organized, well-supported essay.

The 4-Step Method for Writing Essays

STEP 1 **Introduce** the topic, and then write a thesis statement that takes a clear and definite position. (introductory paragraph)

STEP 2 **Support** your thesis statement with reasons and details. (body paragraphs)

STEP 3 **Restate** your thesis, and plug it back into the topic. (concluding paragraph)

STEP 4 **Proofread** what you have written for spelling, grammar, vocabulary, and sentence structure.

It All Adds Up
Writing mechanics such as spelling, grammar, punctuation, and vocabulary are important components of your essay.

Try It Out!

What mnemonic device can you think of to help you remember the steps of this method?

_____

_____

_____

_____

Writing the Introduction

The Topic Sentence

The topic of your essay is the subject you have been asked to write about. Topics are extremely general categories: football, war, jobs, cooking, movies, Gandhi's life, and so on.

Your first job as an essay writer is to introduce this topic in an interesting, engaging way. Imagine that your reader **has not read the essay prompt.** It is up to *you* to set the stage.

The Thesis Statement

The thesis tells readers what your essay will be about *specifically*. It comes at the end of your introductory paragraph.

If the essay question asks you to explain how to cook a simple meal, your topic sentence might be about the renewed interest in cooking at home. Your thesis statement might be, "Chili is a simple and tasty dish that even beginners can cook."

If the essay question asks you to describe an unforgettable character, your topic sentence might be about how varied and interesting people are. Your thesis statement might be, "My fourth-grade teacher was one of the strangest people I ever met."

The Bridge

Getting from the topic sentence to the thesis statement can be tricky. Don't simply jump. Take a few sentences to work your way there. Lead your reader from the general to the specific.

Try It Out!

Write an introductory paragraph for the following essay question.

Should students be required to say the Pledge of Allegiance in school each morning?

_____

_____

_____

_____

Loud and Clear
A thesis statement should be understandable, unambiguous, and provable. It should tell readers exactly what the rest of the essay will be about.

Reasons and Details

Reasons

Reasons can be many things, depending on the kind of thesis statement you have written.

If you are explaining a state of affairs, reasons clarify *why* that state came about:

> Causes of the Civil War included the precarious <u>balance of congressional power between slave states and free states</u>, <u>an imbalance of economic power between North and South</u>, and the <u>moral issue of slavery</u>.

If you are outlining a process, reasons are the steps that make up the whole:

> To make scrambled eggs, you must <u>break the eggs</u>, <u>mix them</u>, and then <u>cook them</u>.

If you are describing an object or a person, reasons are the different aspects on which you want to focus:

> Gandhi <u>led the Indian people to independence</u> through his commitment to <u>nonviolent</u> but <u>direct-action</u> protest against the ruling British.

Details

Details are the examples, illustrations, quotes, statistics, or arguments that support your reasons.

If you are explaining a state of affairs:

> As the country expanded westward, each new state admitted to the union added pro-slavery or anti-slavery representatives to Congress.

If you are outlining a process:

> To avoid getting bits of shell in your egg mixture, crack the egg once quickly.

If you are describing an object or a person:

> Gandhi started his life as a small-time lawyer, showing that anyone with passion for a cause can become a leader.

Try It Out!

Supply one reason and two details for the thesis statement you wrote on page 202.

Reason: _____

Detail: _____

_____

Detail: _____

_____

Noted
Don't write complete sentences here. This is just a note-taking exercise.

Putting It All Together

Always take time to organize your thoughts before you write. You may think that this is a waste of time, but it's not. If you start writing without knowing where you are going, you will just have to spend more time rewriting later. An outline can be very helpful; it gives you a skeleton of what you are going to write. Once you have a good outline, the actual writing becomes much simpler.

Create a chart for yourself, with room to fill in all of the important elements of the essay: your thesis, your reasons, and your details:

Thesis Statement	Reasons and Details
	Reason 1:
	Detail 1:
	Detail 2:
	Reason 2:
	Detail 1:
	Detail 2:

Make Room for Details
If you have more reasons and more details—great! Just make your chart bigger to make room for them.

You should always have *at least* two reason paragraphs in the body of your essay and *at least* two details to support each reason.

Why? Because one reason or detail can be a strange fluke—a one-time-only thing. If you have at least two pieces of evidence on your side, you make a stronger argument.

Try It Out!

Use the outline chart above to outline a response to the essay question from page 202.

Should students be required to say the Pledge of Allegiance in school each morning?

Writing the Conclusion

You have written an introduction. You have outlined your reasons and details so that the body will be easy to write. Now what?

Now it's time for the Big Finish.

A good essay should have a good ending. Without a strong conclusion, even a well-written essay will feel as though it has run out of steam at the end.

What should a conclusion do?

A good, strong conclusion does three things.

1. It restates the thesis.

Go back to the introduction and remind readers what you set out to prove or show. *Don't* tell readers why are you are doing this. "As you can see…," "Thus, I have proven…," and "As I said…" are clunky and obvious. A simple restatement is clear enough. Readers will understand why you are doing it.

2. It summarizes the reasons and details.

In a sentence or two, remind readers what your main reasons have been. Don't use exactly the same wording you used in the body, and don't take too long. A brief recap is all that is needed here.

3. It points forward.

As you tie up the essay and prepare to say good-bye, what do you want your readers to take away? Does your argument lead to a proposal for future action? Does your explanation of a process lead to a vote of confidence that readers can accomplish the process themselves? Does your description lead to some opinion about what has been described? Make readers feel that your essay is not only interesting, but is also useful and relevant.

Color By Numbers
First, tell readers what you are going to tell them. Then tell them that thing. Then tell them what you told them. It seems simple, maybe even silly, but it works.

Try It Out!

Write a concluding paragraph to the essay you outlined on page 205.

_____

_____

_____

_____

_____

_____

_____

Say It New
Restate your ideas in the conclusion; don't recopy things word for word.

The Final Step

Step 4 of the 4-Step Method tells you to proofread. This step is every bit as important as the other three. When your writing is flawed, people often assume that your thinking is flawed.

Proofread for:

- misspelled words
- run-on sentences
- sentence fragments
- punctuation errors
- subject-verb agreement
- tense agreement

Try It Out!

Proofread the following paragraph, and circle any errors that you find.

Some people might says that these are risks are proof that students should stay far away from political or social cause. However it is exactly this risk of failure or compromise that make social action important for students how are young people supposed to learn the seriousness of real-world issues and the difficulty of making the right decisions unless they can see their ideas? And put into action? How, can students learn to respect the choices made by their elders if they didn't ever get a taste of how difficult it is to made those choices?

Your Essay is You
Proofreading helps you make a good impression. The only thing the test scorers know about you is what you write.

Guided Practice

Create an outline for the following essay question.

Should parents be allowed to monitor and restrict Internet use for their high school-aged children?

Thesis Statement	Reasons and Details
Take a firm position on this topic.	Reason 1: Explain why you feel the way you do. Detail 1: Supply some evidence or argument why your reason is correct. Detail 2: Reason 2: Detail 1: Detail 2:

Connections
Don't forget to use transition words to link your ideas and sentences. Help move your readers from idea to idea.

Independent Practice

Create an outline for the following essay question.

Writing Task

Think about a technical process with which you are familiar. Think about your hobbies and interests. Do you cook? Do you sew? Can you make things from wood or clay? Do you write? Can you assemble electronic equipment? What can you make, build, or do that many other people would find difficult to accomplish? Think carefully about the steps involved in making or doing this thing.

Write a composition in which you describe this technical process. Explain step-by-step how to work through this process to achieve the desired end.

Thesis Statement	Reasons and Details
	Reason 1:
	Detail 1:
	Detail 2:
	Reason 2:
	Detail 1:
	Detail 2:

✓HINT Don't forget to supply supporting information for every reason you give. Without details, you will be left with one-sentence body paragraphs!

Write the introduction and conclusion for this essay.

Introduction

_____

_____

_____

_____

_____

_____

_____

Conclusion

_____

_____

_____

_____

_____

_____

_____

Test Practice

Write an essay in response to the following question.

REMINDER

- Write your response to the writing prompt below.
- You may give your writing a title if you like, but it is not necessary.
- You may NOT use a dictionary. If you do not know how to spell a word, sound the word out, and do the best you can.
- You may either print or write in cursive.
- Write clearly! Any erasures or strike-throughs should be as clean as possible.

Writing Task

> Think about historical figures you have found interesting or intriguing. If you could have dinner with any historical figure, whom would you choose, and why? What would you talk about? What would you want to ask him or her?
>
> Write an essay in which you explain why you would like to meet this person and what you would want to ask him or her.
>
> Checklist for Your Writing
>
> The following checklist will help you do your best work. Make sure you:
>
> ☐ Read the task carefully.
>
> ☐ Use specific details and examples to demonstrate your understanding.
>
> ☐ Organize your writing with a strong introduction, body, and conclusion.
>
> ☐ Choose a style, tone, and vocabulary that are appropriate for your audience and purpose.
>
> ☐ Vary your sentences to make your writing interesting to read.
>
> ☐ Check for mistakes in grammar, spelling, punctuation, and sentence structure.

Unit 9 ReKAP

- The mnemonic, "I Supplied Real Proof," reminds me that the 4-Step Method tells me first to _____ the topic, then to _____, then _____, and finally _____.

- Before writing my essay, I will create an outline chart with room for the _____ and my _____ and _____.

- After writing my first draft, I will be sure to proofread, checking _____, _____, _____, _____, and _____.

WRITING A RESPONSE TO LITERATURE

Thinking KAP

Tell the story of your favorite book in one sentence, one paragraph, and two paragraphs. The one-paragraph version should *not* continue what the one-sentence version has started; each version should be complete in itself and should adequately sum up your favorite book within the space given.

What must you omit to sum up your favorite book in a sentence? What will you include in the two-paragraph version that you had to omit in the one-paragraph version?

One Sentence:

_____

One Paragraph:

_____

_____

_____

_____

_____

Two Paragraphs:

_____

_____

_____

_____

_____

_____

_____

_____

_____

A Response to Literature Essay

As you saw in Unit 9, your CAHSEE essay question can be one of several types. We have already looked at how to write an essay in response to a question (prompt). The one type of essay we haven't looked at yet is a Response to Literature. We saved it for last because it requires all of the skills you have learned and practiced in this course.

▷ What skills are involved in writing an essay in response to literature?

_____

_____

_____

Hints Abound

Look at the kinds of questions the test makers are asking about the passage. The multiple-choice questions can help you get an understanding of the test makers' feelings and attitudes towards the passage. This can often be helpful in framing your essay.

Return of the 4-Step Method

The basics of good essay writing remain the same, whether you are responding to a writing prompt or a text-based question. To outline and plan your essay, use the 4-Step Method for Writing Essays that you learned in Unit 9.

**The 4-Step Method
for Writing Essays**

Step **1** **Introduce** the topic, and then write a thesis statement that takes a clear and definite position. (introductory paragraph)

Step **2** **Support** your thesis statement with reasons and details. (body paragraphs)

Step **3** **Restate** your thesis, and plug it back into the topic. (concluding paragraph)

Step **4** **Proofread** what you have written for spelling, grammar, vocabulary, and sentence structure.

No Right Answer?
Response to Literature questions are not as arbitrary or open-ended as they may seem. Answers *must* be connected strongly to the text, even if they require extensions *beyond* the text.

The CAHSEE may ask you to do one of two things with a text.

You may be asked to **analyze** the text.

▷ What does it mean to analyze something?

_____

Or you may be asked to make an **extension beyond** the text.

▷ What does it mean to make an extension beyond something?

_____

© 2006 Kaplan, Inc.

Analyzing

A Response to Literature essay question may ask you to *analyze* information from a text. In such a question, you will be asked not only to supply an answer, but also to *judge* it using information from the passage. What is the author's purpose or point of view? Why is one detail better or more important than another detail? Why did one character make the choice she made? What will be the result of an action or trend being described?

Each of these questions requires you to make a choice based on what you have read. Once you have made your choice, use the 4-Step Method you learned in Unit 9 to flesh out the response.

Try It Out!

Read the following passage. Then turn the page to answer the essay question.

Acid Rain

One of today's most challenging environmental problems is acid rain. Heavy industry routinely disperses acid into the air, a development that can have terrible consequences. If these acids are not destroyed by natural chemicals in the ground, they can accumulate and destroy various types of animals and plants. In some parts of the American Northeast and Midwest, ten percent of all lakes have dangerous acid levels, threatening their aquatic populations. In eastern mountains, large forests have been severely damaged because trees are regularly bathed in acidic clouds.

Acid rain is caused by factories and power plants that release compounds of nitrogen and sulfur. When these harmful elements combine with clean air, the result is the creation of menacing acids. The pollutants most often come from oil- and coal-burning factories and power plants. Though the damage caused by acid rain is often not obvious at first, it becomes discernable over time.

To reduce acid rain, smoke from these factories and power plants must be made less toxic. One inexpensive and quick method to decrease the amount of chemical pollutants pumped into the atmosphere is to install machines that remove these pollutants from a factory's or plant's exhaust system. A second, more elaborate method is to build entirely new factories or plants based on experimental designs that produce less acidic fallout. Only by choosing one of these methods will we be able to safeguard plant and animal life in our country.

Never Walk Alone
If you find that there is no information in the passage to support the choice you have made, it is probably the wrong choice! Go back and choose an answer for which there is more support.

Writing Task:

The article proposes two solutions to the problem of acid rain. Which solution would provide the most dramatic short-term results? Which solution would make the most sense in the long term?

Write an essay in which you evaluate the two solutions offered by the author.

Use details and examples from the passage.

Thesis Statement	Reasons and Details
	Reason 1:
	Detail 1:
	Detail 2:
	Reason 2:
	Detail 1:
	Detail 2:

Going Beyond

The second type of Response to Literature question asks you to use your imagination to extend information from the reading passage into a different situation or scenario.

The challenge of these questions is to stay connected to the passage. What information have you been given that would be relevant or useful in the new situation you have been asked to imagine? How does the main idea of the passage translate into this new situation?

Stay focused on the 2Ws, and think about what changes and what stays the same when they shift over into the new scenario.

Try It Out!

George Gray

by EDGAR LEE MASTERS

Line
1   I have studied many times
     The marble which was chiseled for me—
     A boat with a furled sail at rest in a harbor.
     In truth it pictures not my destination
5   But my life.
     For love was offered me and I shrank from its disillusionment;
     Sorrow knocked at my door, but I was afraid;
     Ambition called to me, but I dreaded the chances.
     Yet all the while I hungered for meaning in my life.
10 And now I know that we must lift the sail
     And catch the winds of destiny
     Wherever they drive the boat.
     To put meaning in one's life may end in madness,
     But life without meaning is the torture
15 Of restlessness and vague desire—
     It is a boat longing for the sea and yet afraid.

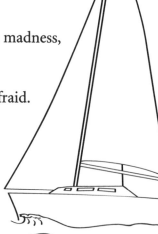

Writing Task:

What important advice does the poem "George Gray" have for young people preparing to graduate from high school and face the world?

What does the author think of the life choices that George Gray has made? What message or lesson do those choices have for teenagers?

Write a composition that gives advice to high school seniors preparing to graduate, using details and examples from the poem to support your main ideas.

Stay in the Ballpark
An easy pitfall of "Go Beyond" questions is to wander off topic. Keep your eyes on the main idea of the text, and make sure that your answer stays in the ballpark.

Thesis Statement	Reasons and Details
	Reason 1:
	Detail 1:
	Detail 2:
	Reason 2:
	Detail 1:
	Detail 2:

Guided Practice

School-Based Management

There have been many efforts at school reform in America. Read this essay and learn about one idea that seeks to restructure the way schools are run.

School-Based Management (SBM) may be the most significant educational reform in decades, and yet no two people agree on what it is, how to achieve it, or even why to do it at all. Defining SBM, therefore, is somewhat problematic. One short definition is "democratic administration." More specifically, SBM is an attempt to transform schools into communities where all the affected parties are involved in making important decisions. No longer the traditional top-down school management structure, SBM requires administrators, teachers, parents, and even students to become connected to the decision-making process.

The reasons for implementing SBM are varied, but the bottom line for most of them is that SBM can enhance student achievement. In an ideal setting, this seems logical. Teachers and parents, who are in direct contact with students on a daily basis, get a say in curricular goals, disciplinary action, and other important decisions. Administrators provide a district-wide perspective that allows for a cohesive learning experience as students proceed through grade levels. The driving theory behind SBM is that everybody can focus on student learning. Of course, not every theory is perfect in reality. Many questions surrounding SBM remain unanswered. How much decision-making power does each party get? Who decides the balance of power? How does SBM function in an emergency situation?

Even with these pertinent questions, SBM is a rapidly growing system of school administration. The most recognizable seeds of this reform appeared approximately 16 years ago when the National Commission on Excellence in Education suggested a restructuring of schools and districts. However, the concept of democratic administration was evident at the beginning of the twentieth century. In 1903, John Dewey wrote, "Until the public school system is organized in such a way that every teacher has some regular and representative way…[to] register judgment upon matters of educational importance,…the assertion that the present system is not…democratic seems to be justified."

© 2006 Kaplan, Inc.

The grounds for democracy in education gained strength during the 1960s. A 1966 report from the National Association of Secondary-School Principals stated that the best education of students demands a genuine working partnership of teachers, principals, superintendents, and school boards. This view was maintained, though not officially implemented, throughout the 1970s. The National Institute of Education completed a study in 1977 concluding that schools must integrate teachers and the community into decision-making. The 1980s saw the appearance of SBM itself and the beginnings of policy recommending its implementation into the school structure.

What gave SBM its widest ranging acceptance was the decentralization of power and decision-making in the private sector during the 1990s. As business leaders discovered the competitive and economic advantages of sharing power and knowledge, the idea of decentralization became more widely accepted and popular. Successful companies have found that granting decision-making power to teams or team leaders has given employees a greater stake in the success of the business and has given businesses a deeper and wider pool of creativity upon which to draw.

The sharing of knowledge has been key to American business in the last decade as well, and this knowledge is not limited to facts and details about the company's work. Employees have been encouraged to pursue extensive training while on the job, to deepen and broaden their skills. No longer are employees hired to do one thing and expected to continue doing that one thing forever. Employees at successful businesses are encouraged to take initiative, learn more, and do more—again maximizing the creative potential of the workforce.

Business in America has discovered that innovation—the next big idea that will change everything—may come from any place within the workforce. A business that shuts its ears to the majority of its employees only stands to hurt itself. The old stereotype of big business, with its czar-like executives and its faceless drones at rows of identical desks, is now as outdated in corporate America as the typewriter.

Interestingly, the public sector has proven more resistant to this kind of change. SBM continues to be talked about, argued over, and, in some places, implemented. What role it will play in the future of American schooling remains to be seen.

Scan First
Don't forget to scan the question on page 230 first. Find out *why* you need to read the passage. Let the question focus your reading.

Writing Task:

> What arguments could you present to a local board of education in favor of implementing school-based management in your community's schools?

▷ What choice are you being asked to make?

_____

▷ What information can help you defend that choice?

_____

_____

_____

Thesis Statement	Reasons and Details
	Reason 1:
	Detail 1:
	Detail 2:
	Reason 2:
	Detail 1:
	Detail 2:

Independent Practice

Read this passage, and answer the essay question on page 232.

A Young Woman Remembers

Heavens, we've been out of the Dark Ages for nearly two centuries, and still men treat us abominably if we women show any inclination of a mind of our own. It's simply not fair that my brother, who isn't all that talented, receives most of my father's attention in teaching us his painting trade. Of course, when I was young, he wanted me to learn to draw. It  was an important accomplishment, along with singing, playing an instrument, and knowing how to turn a fine stitch with a needle. But to Papa, my artistic talent was just another asset for attracting a future husband. That's all he cares about for me really. That I marry. Of course, without a husband I can't survive, since men hold all the economic and political power.

Still, after years of working in the studio alongside Papa and my brother, I know that art is more than a frivolous pastime with which to entertain potential mates. It is as rigorous as reading and writing, which my tutor taught me as a small child. My brother said that philosophy and studying languages was more challenging, but girls are not allowed to learn these subjects, so I can't compare them to art. But after countless hours in the studio, I can mix paints expertly, fill backgrounds, and frame the pictures my father makes for patrons. I was forbidden to sketch live male nudes when my brother drew from the model. I've learned instead to draw the human body by studying women, my friends, and family. If I get stuck on male anatomy, I look back at some earlier master's painting to understand his approach.

Papa's pressuring me to marry and settle down to raise the eleven or so children I'm bound to have once wed. The only way he will allow me to paint professionally is if I agree to have a family—and let him take all the money I make from my pictures. It hardly seems right. My brother now has gone to join the painter's guild and will be assured clients and a steady income of his own. But the smell of paint and the feel of the brush on canvas call me too strongly, and I will agree to father's terms.

© 2006 Kaplan, Inc.

Writing Task:

In this young woman's memoir, the author describes the difficulties she has had in pursuing a career as an artist. In each paragraph, she supports her main purpose in writing. What is the author's purpose for writing this memoir? What details does she give to support her purpose?

Write an essay in which you discuss the author's purpose in writing this memoir.

Write your introduction here:

_____

_____

_____

_____

_____

_____

_____

Write your conclusion here:

_____

_____

_____

_____

_____

_____

_____

Test Practice

You read this selection in Unit 6. Read it again, and answer the essay question that follows.

Jurgis Underground

by UPTON SINCLAIR

> Upton Sinclair's *The Jungle* was a groundbreaking expose of working conditions in America in the early part of the 20th century. In this excerpt, a man named Jurgis discovers the dangers of working under the streets of the city.

The tunnel was a peculiar one for telephone wires; it was about eight feet high, and with a level floor nearly as wide. It had innumerable branches—a perfect spider web beneath the city; Jurgis walked over half a mile with his gang to the place where they were to work. Stranger yet, the tunnel was lighted by electricity, and upon it was laid a double-tracked, narrow-gauge railroad!

It was in a newly opened cut that Jurgis worked, and so he knew that he had an all-winter job. He was so rejoiced that he treated himself to a spree that night, and with the balance of his money he hired himself a place in a tenement room, where he slept upon a big homemade straw mattress along with four other workingmen. This was one dollar a week, and for four more he got his food in a boardinghouse near his work. This would leave him four dollars extra each week, an unthinkable sum for him. At the outset he had to pay for his digging tools, and also to buy a pair of heavy boots, since his shoes were falling to pieces, and a flannel shirt, since the one he had worn all summer was in shreds. He spent a week meditating whether or not he should also buy an overcoat. There was one belonging to a collar button peddler, who had died in the room next to him, and which the landlady was holding for her rent; in the end, however, Jurgis decided to do without it, as he was to be underground by day and in bed at night.

On an average, the tunneling cost a life a day and several manglings; it was seldom, however, that more than a dozen or two men heard of any one accident. The work was all done by the new boring machinery, with as little blasting as possible; but there would be falling rocks and crushed supports, and premature explosions—and in addition all the dangers of railroading. So it was that one night, as Jurgis was on his way out with his gang, an engine and a loaded car dashed round one of the innumerable right-angle branches and struck him upon the shoulder, hurling him against the concrete wall and knocking him senseless.

When he opened his eyes again it was to the clanging of the bell of an ambulance. He was lying in it, covered by a blanket, and it was threading its way slowly through the holiday-shopping crowds. They took him to the county hospital, where a young surgeon set his arm; then he was washed and laid upon a bed in a ward with a score or two more of maimed and mangled men.

Jurgis was ready to leave the hospital at the end of two weeks. This did not mean that his arm was strong and that he was able to go back to work, but simply that he could get along without further attention, and that his place was needed for some one worse off than he. That he was utterly helpless, and had no means of keeping himself alive in the meantime, was something which did not concern the hospital authorities, nor any one else in the city.

As it chanced, he had been hurt on a Monday, and had just paid for his last week's board and his room rent, and spent nearly all the balance of his Saturday's pay. He had less than seventy-five cents in his pockets, and a dollar and a half due him for the day's work he had done before he was hurt. He might possibly have sued the company, and got some damages for his injuries, but he did not know this, and it was not the company's business to tell him.

So Jurgis went out into the streets, in a most dreadful plight. It was bitterly cold, and a heavy snow was falling, beating into his face. He had no overcoat, and no place to go, and two dollars and sixty-five cents in his pocket, with the certainty that he could not earn another cent for months. Words could not paint the terror that came over him as he realized all this. There would be no consideration for him because of his weakness—it was no one's business to help him in such distress, to make the fight the least bit easier for him. He was like a wounded animal in the forest; he was forced to compete with his enemies upon unequal terms.

Writing Task:

What is the author's attitude towards Jurgis and his predicament? How do the author's tone and choice of words reveal his point of view?

Write an essay in which you discuss the author's point of view and the strategies he uses for communicating it.

What details and examples does he use to support his point of view?

Checklist for Your Writing

The following checklist will help you do your best work. Make sure you:

- ☐ Read the passage and the task carefully.

- ☐ Use specific details and examples from the passage to demonstrate your understanding of the author's point of view and attitude.

- ☐ Organize your writing with a strong introduction, body, and conclusion.

- ☐ Choose a style, tone, and vocabulary that are appropriate for your audience and purpose.

- ☐ Vary your sentences to make your writing interesting to read.

- ☐ Check for mistakes in grammar, spelling, punctuation, and sentence structure.

Name _____ Date _____

_____

_____

_____

_____

_____

_____

_____

_____

_____

_____

_____

_____

_____

_____

_____

_____

_____

_____

_____

_____

_____

_____

_____

Unit 10 ReKAP

Look back at the strategies in this unit, and review them. Then fill in the spaces below to show what you have learned.

- To answer a Response to Literature essay question on the CAHSEE, I will use

   the _____ Method.

- For questions requiring **analysis**, I will make sure to supply clear

   _____ for every position I take.

- For questions requiring an **extension** beyond the text, I will remember to

   remain focused on the _____ and stay in the _____.

FULL-LENGTH PRACTICE TEST

Full-Length Practice Test

You are about to take the CAHSEE Full-Length Practice Test in English-Language Arts. Before beginning work on the test, review these important test-taking strategies.

Predicting

Avoid falling victim to distracting answer choices. Cover the answers with your hand and match the best choice to your prediction.

Eliminating

While you should not spend too much time on any one question, you should try to answer every question on the test. If you're stuck, rule out the answer choices that you know are wrong. Make an educated guess from those that remain.

Pacing

Don't let one question eat up all your time. You want to move through the CAHSEE at a steady pace, even though the test is untimed. Scan the multiple-choice questions and then read the passage with an eye towards the main idea. Don't linger on the details; you can return to the passage later while answering detail-oriented questions.

Skipping Around

Do not feel chained to the order in which information is presented to you. Unless you see a sign that says, "Stop," feel free to skip passages that look difficult and read easier selections first. Within a passage, you can skip the questions that look difficult and score the easier points first. Having some points under your belt always increases your confidence.

Take a Deep Breath
It's important to relax when taking the CAHSEE. Don't worry about questions that have stumped you. Concentrate on the ones you know you can answer and do the best you can.

CAHSEE Full-Length Practice Test in English-Language Arts

This test is made up of two sessions. Each session should take you approximately two hours. Today you will complete Session 1. When your teacher tells you to start, you may turn the page and begin working.

Session 1

The following article about an important event in United States history. Read "The Gold Rush" and answer questions 1 through 5.

The Gold Rush

It lasted less than ten years, but when it was over, the United States had been radically and forever changed. The population had exploded on the west coast of the country, fortunes had been made and lost, and a new state had entered the union—California.

The United States acquired the territory that would later become California during the United States-Mexican War (1846–1848). One of the many settlers who traveled to the new territory was John Sutter, a shopkeeper from Switzerland who had left behind his wife, his children, and his debts in search of a new life. He hired a carpenter named James Marshall to build a sawmill for him on the American River in the foothills of the Sierra Nevada mountains.

On January 24, 1848, while inspecting the mill's runoff into the river, Marshall saw two shiny objects below the surface of the water. Gold! He took the nuggets to Sutter, who was annoyed by the discovery; he did not want his mill workers distracted by "gold fever." He kept the discovery quiet for a while, but then could not resist bragging about it. As news spread, workers began quitting their jobs and heading into the hills to look for the source of the gold that had washed down the river. The Gold Rush had officially begun.

Ironically, the man who discovered the gold never made any money from it. Marshall tried to lay claim to the land near Sutter's Mill, but other people moved in and took over the land, forcing him to abandon his claim. He tried

to find gold in other places, and he even told people that he had supernatural, gold-finding powers. He ended up fleeing and died an impoverished man.

Sutter also fell on hard times. He had to sell his sawmill to pay his debts. He bought a farm in another part of the Gold Rush country, but fires and floods destroyed it. He eventually moved east and was forgotten.

In the meantime, people sojourned to California by the thousands in search of fortune and glory. During the two years after Marshall's discovery, more than 90,000 people made their way to California, looking for gold. So many people moved west during 1849 that all of the prospectors (regardless of when they arrived) became known as Forty-Niners. By 1850, so many people had moved to the California territory that the United States Congress was forced to declare it a new state. In 1854, the population had increased by another 300,000 people. One out of every 90 people then living in the United States was living in California.

The Gold Rush was not limited to California, either. The allure of gold brought people to Alaska, Arizona, Idaho, Montana, Nevada, New Mexico, South Dakota, Utah, and Wyoming. The Gold Rush created new cities and new states, new systems of transportation, and new economies. Some people found gold and became rich. Others failed in their quest for gold, but then became farmers and ranchers in California's Central Valley.

The appeal of the Gold Rush also attracted people from all over the world who were in search of wealth. In late 1849, there were ships in San Francisco Bay bearing the flags of Belgium, Chile, England, France, Germany, Hawaii, Mexico, Norway, Peru, Portugal, Russia, Spain, Sweden, and Tahiti. From its very birth, California was one of the most ethnically and culturally diverse regions on earth.

Simply arriving in California was no guarantee of success. Mining was difficult, dangerous, and backbreaking work. One scholar estimated that one of every five miners who arrived in California in 1849 died within six months from the intense labor involved.

As the gold began to disappear, suspicion and hostility erupted as people struggled to survive. Acts of targeted violence against African Americans, Chinese Americans, and Native Americans exploded, and anti-immigrant sentiments began to flare up throughout the state. By 1854, the Gold Rush was over, and the new state of California plunged into an economic depression.

However, even after all of the gold had been taken from the ground, and the state came through its turbulent times, California remained a magical place in the imagination of many. The thirty-first state had become a place thought of as somewhere that dreams could come true.

1. **Which statement BEST summarizes the author's main point?**

   A   This article was written to explain what happened to John Sutter and James Marshall.

   B   This article was developed to describe how the California Gold Rush began.

   C   This article was developed to point out how people's greed can affect history.

   D   This article was written to trace the rise and fall of the Gold Rush.

2. **Which of the following is NOT a correct rewording of the following sentence?**

   > In the meantime, people sojourned to California by the thousands in search of fortune and glory.

   A   Meanwhile, thousands of people traveled to California in search of fortune and glory.

   B   Meanwhile, thousands of people trekked to California in search of fortune and glory.

   C   Meanwhile, thousands of people expedited to California in search of fortune and glory.

   D   Meanwhile, thousands of people voyaged to California in search of fortune and glory.

3. **There was probably an increase in violence towards the end of the Gold Rush because—**

   A   people were frustrated that there was no more gold to be found.

   B   ethnic minorities had no legal rights to gold.

   C   people were angry about the hard work related to mining.

   D   there was a depression in California.

4. **The passage provides the LEAST information on—**

   A   the United States-Mexican War.

   B   population changes in the United States.

   C   the draw of the Gold Rush.

   D   mining conditions.

5.
   > The allure of gold brought people to Alaska, Arizona, Idaho, Montana, Nevada, New Mexico, South Dakota, Utah, and Wyoming.

   In this sentence from the article, the word *allure* means—

   A   danger.

   B   totality.

   C   appeal.

   D   cost.

Read this poem and answer questions 6 through 9.

Sonnet XXIX
by Elizabeth Barrett Browning

> Born in England in 1806, Elizabeth Barrett Browning developed an early interest in the plays of William Shakespeare, the histories and writings of Greece and Rome, and poetry. She was one of the most highly-regarded female poets among readers in the United States and England during the nineteenth century.

1   I think of thee!—my thoughts do twine and bud
    About thee, as wild vines, about a tree,
    Put out broad leaves, and soon there's nought to see
    Except the straggling green which hides the wood.
5   Yet, O my palm-tree, be it understood
    I will not have my thoughts instead of thee
    Who art dearer, better! Rather, instantly
    Renew thy presence; as a strong tree should,
    Rustle thy boughs and set thy trunk all bare,
10 And let these bands of greenery which insphere thee,
    Drop heavily down,—burst, shattered everywhere!
    Because, in this deep joy to see and hear thee
    And breathe within thy shadow a new air,
    I do not think of thee—I am too near thee.

6. **What is the theme of the poem?**

   A the calm of gardens

   B finding joy in another person

   C the strength of trees

   D revitalizing a broken friendship

7. **The poet compares her loved one to a—**

   A vine.

   B tree.

   C rose.

   D leaf.

8. **In line 10, *insphere* means—**

   A encircle.

   B enshrine.

   C enmesh.

   D entice.

9. **How might the author's background be reflected in the poem?**

   A The poem shows why the author became a writer.

   B The poem shows that the author knew Shakespeare personally.

   C The poem describes how the author became interested in Shakespeare.

   D The poem demonstrates an understanding of Shakespearean metaphors.

Read this passage and answer questions 10 through 12.

Two Kinds of Tragedy

Certain of William Shakespeare's plays are classified as "tragedies," but they are very different from the ancient Greek form of theatre that bears the same name.

Shakespeare's dramas are similar to the Greek plays in that both types end badly for the main characters. But a tragedy, according to the Greeks who invented the form, should focus solely on the fall from grace of a king or some other noble or highborn character. This fall is almost always the result of a "tragic flaw" in the main character's personality.

In Shakespeare, on the other hand, the tragic end is not always the result of a character's mistake or flaw. Rather, the tragedy often seems to come from a disturbance of the "natural order of things." When that order is disturbed, chaos and destruction will result until the natural order is restored. Thus, innocent people can be swept away by events beyond their control. Their fates are not always the result of actions or decisions they have made.

In addition, the Greek plays take place in a single setting over a controlled period of time—usually the span of a single day. Shakespeare's plays occur in locations all over the earth and can cover many years. Although both types of tragedy were extremely popular with their respective audiences, the Greek

plays were especially written to evoke pity and terror as part of a religious festival celebrating the god Dionysus. The terrible events of the plays were meant to show people the nature of fate and their roles in the universe. However, Shakespeare's plays were written for a commercial theatre and were intended strictly as entertainment.

10. **Which of the following sentences from the selection offers the BEST support of the main idea?**

    A   But a tragedy, according to the Greeks who invented the form, should focus solely on the fall from grace of a noble or highborn character.

    B   Although both types of tragedy were extremely popular with their audiences, the Greek plays were written to evoke pity and terror as part of a religious festival celebrating the god Dionysus.

    C   In Shakespeare, on the other had, the tragic end is not always the result of a character's mistake or flaw.

    D   Certain of William Shakespeare's plays are classified as "tragedies," but they are very different from the ancient Greek form of theatre that bears the same name.

11. **Read this sentence from the selection.**

    > When that order is disturbed, chaos and destruction will result until the natural order is restored.

    What does the word *restored* mean in this sentence from the passage?

    A   purposed

    B   removed

    C   suppressed

    D   returned

12. **Which of the following statements BEST describes the essential difference between Greek and Shakespearean tragedy?**

    A   The main character in Greek tragedy comes to a bad end.

    B   Shakespearean tragic heroes always deserve their fate.

    C   Greek tragedies were not as popular as Shakespeare's.

    D   Shakespeare's plays were not part of a religious festival.

Read this passage and answer questions 13 through 16.

The Mysterious Planet X

The remotest planet of our solar system is Pluto. It was discovered by astronomer Clyde W. Tombaugh in 1930. Earlier in the century, an astronomer named Percival Lowell had predicted the existence of a planet beyond Neptune. Lowell had believed that certain irregularities in the orbit of Uranus were being caused by an unknown Planet X. Years later, Tombaugh began searching for Planet X at the Arizona observatory named for Lowell. A careful sky survey led to the discovery of the new, distant planet. The new planet was named Pluto.

In Roman mythology, Pluto is the god of the underworld. The ninth planet may have gotten this odd name because it is so far from the Sun that it is eternally in darkness. It may also have been given this name because "PL" are the initials of Percival Lowell.

Pluto is only five-hundredths of the size of Earth. Pluto is not only smaller than all the other planets, it is smaller than most of the moons in our solar system. In fact, after Tombaugh's discovery, it was determined that Pluto was too small to account for the discrepancies Lowell had found in the orbits of the other planets. Because of this, some astronomers believe that the mysterious Planet X may still be out there somewhere beyond Pluto, waiting to be discovered. Others have come to think that Pluto may not be a planet at all, but is instead a satellite of Neptune that simply lost its way in the cosmos.

For all of our scientific advances, Pluto is still very much a mystery to us. It is the only planet that has not been visited by a spacecraft, and even the Hubble Space Telescope can only make out the largest features of the planet's surface.

Little is known about Pluto's composition and atmosphere. The planet is most likely composed of rock and ice. The atmosphere probably consists of nitrogen, with some carbon monoxide and methane. It is possible that Pluto's atmosphere is gaseous only when Pluto's orbit brings it closest to the sun. For the majority of Pluto's long year, the atmospheric gases may well be frozen solid.

Even Pluto's orbit is strange. The planet does not travel in the same direction as most of the other planets, and its path occasionally brings it closer to the sun than the planet Neptune's does.

Pluto has one satellite, named Charon, which was not discovered until 1978. Charon is named for the mythological figure who ferried the dead across the River Styx into Hades, the underworld. Before Charon was discovered, most astronomers thought that Pluto was much larger than it is. They did not realize that the blurry image they were seeing was actually two separate objects. In fact, Charon is so close to the size of Pluto that some people do not even consider it a moon. They prefer to think of Pluto and Charon as a double planet.

Science fiction stories love to talk about traveling to strange and distant galaxies, but in fact our own galactic neighborhood is still profoundly mysterious to us.

13. **Which one of the following themes is developed in the article?**

   A   the exploration of the unknown

   B   the debate over changing details

   C   the advances of astronomy

   D   the effects on the universe

14. **Why did astronomers once think that Pluto was larger than it actually is?**

   A   The Hubble Telescope can make out only large features.

   B   Pluto's atmosphere is gaseous and large only part of the time.

   C   Pluto's blurry image obscured some vital information.

   D   The astronomers made mathematical miscalculations.

15. **Which of the following is NOT a correct rewording of the following sentence?**

> It was determined that Pluto was too small to account for the discrepancies Lowell had found in the orbits of the other planets.

   A   Pluto's small size could not justify the effects on the orbits of other planets.

   B   Pluto's small size could not compromise the effects on the orbits of other planets.

   C   Pluto's small size could not explain the effects on the orbits of other planets.

   D   Pluto's small size could not rationalize the effects on the orbits of other planets.

16. **This article provides the MOST information on—**

   A   astronomy.

   B   Percival Lowell.

   C   the ninth planet.

   D   Charon.

Read this passage on volunteerism and answer questions 17 through 20.

The Volunteerism Debate

Working well with volunteers can be tricky. At first glance, nothing appears more tempting than adding free help to an overtaxed work environment. Any extra assistance might seem as if it would decrease the workload. But a great deal of time and energy must go into preparing and supervising volunteers to ensure that they are truly helpful. A poorly supervised, misguided volunteer can be more harmful than useful.

When recruiting volunteers, it is essential to decide what qualities you are looking for in these people. Decide if they must come to you with specific experience, skills, or training for the tasks you will assign them. Also, will they need to be able to work on their own, or easily collaborate with others as part of a team?

What type of commitment are you seeking? Some volunteers, because they do not receive pay, are tempted to approach their jobs with a careless attitude—showing up whenever they wish, completing tasks at will, and so forth. Ask questions to investigate a person's attitude towards meeting commitments and request references from prospective volunteers.

Once selected, volunteers should not be thrown into a project without a clear understanding of the overall institution and how they fit into the larger picture. Review the organization's mission and services to give volunteers a lay of the land. Volunteers also should clearly understand the chain of command within the office—who reports to whom—as well as to whom they should go when seeking information or assistance.

Training is the next crucial step. Some volunteers come with vast work experience, but it may or may not be exactly relevant to the job at hand. It takes time to teach someone your system, approach, and preferences for the way you want things done. You cannot expect the volunteer to read your mind. Slow and thorough preparation is key.

In training volunteers, it is a good idea to consider the way you want to teach certain skills. Also, consider how you can best communicate with someone who may have some, little, or no background with the job. Think about your own attitudes, as well. Do you have preconceived notions about volunteers? Do you think they are worth less time, consideration, or respect than paid staff? How might differences in age, experience, heritages, or work ethics unconsciously affect the way you interact with them?

Remember you are training a real person, not a generic "volunteer." You are far more likely to get exceptional work from people who feel that you care about them as much as the tasks they are performing.

It is imperative that you have a clear definition of what you want accomplished. Ideally, you and the volunteer should together set down an exact plan for the project; identify necessary resources and agree on a schedule, including times to meet for project updates. Continual short-term review with volunteers about their work will go a long way to getting the results you want.

There is nothing worse than recruiting a promising volunteer—throwing her or him into a project—and weeks or months later seeing the end product for the first time only to discover it was not what you anticipated. This wasted time is avoidable if you check the work along the way from the beginning. Furthermore, frequent reviews allow you to observe the volunteer's skills and, if necessary, scale back or expand the scope of the work.

You should also decide during your planning how you will evaluate the work. Will there be written or verbal feedback? The volunteers should also do self-assessment throughout the process, reflecting on whether they are doing a good job and what they might do to improve their performance.

Assessment by both the volunteer and supervisor will help keep the work on track throughout and also provide a helpful conclusion at the end. Furthermore, both the volunteer and supervisor can use what they learned from the process to help shape future volunteer experiences.

17. **Read this sentence from the selection.**

> Continual short-term review with volunteers about their work will go a long way to getting the results you want.

According to this sentence, employers should—

A   avoid overburdening volunteers.

B   welcome new volunteers whenever they arrive.

C   check in with volunteers once their project is complete.

D   have regular meetings with volunteers.

18. **Why does the author insist that using free assistance from volunteers is not an easy answer to an overburdened office?**

A   Volunteers are not dedicated to their jobs.

B   Supervising volunteers always takes valuable time.

C   Supervising volunteers requires care, time, and planning.

D   Volunteers do not have the skills for the jobs to which they are assigned.

19. **The main purpose of this brochure is—**

A   to explain how to interview volunteers.

B   to explain when to let go of unproductive volunteers.

C   to explain the most effective way to work with volunteers.

D   to explain the best system for attracting new volunteers.

20. **Which of the following would make this selection easier to understand?**

A   a timeline for training and working with volunteer

B   a picture of a volunteer and supervisor

C   a chart with steps to recruiting volunteers

D   an excerpt about a good volunteer experience

Read this story about a young woman and answer questions 21 through 24.

With the Whales

Ana laced up her running shoes and ran through the kitchen, grabbing a roll from the counter. She did not like to run on an empty stomach.

"Bye, Dad!" she called out over her shoulder to her father, who was sitting at the kitchen table reading the newspaper.

"Where are you going? You don't have time to go for a run. You will be late for school, and you can't afford to be tardy again."

"No worries, Dad. I guarantee you I won't be late."

The screen door slammed behind Ana as she ran outside. She turned up the street behind her house and ran up the hill. In front of her, the mountains stretched like a black velvet curtain draped across the sky. The sun had not yet risen over the tops of the volcanic peaks, but just a hint of light peeked from behind the ridge.

This was Ana's favorite part of the day. Soon, the sun would creep over the mountains and flood her side of the island with light, revealing lush sugar cane fields, bright hibiscus flowers, and the turquoise blue ocean. She ascended the hill, making sure she maintained a constant pace, but before the road entered the cane fields, Ana turned around. She let her momentum pull her back down the hill toward the beach— faster and faster. Now she was running through town, striding over curb after curb. She groaned in frustration as she approached the town's main boulevard because the light was red and she would have to stop. She jogged in place and looked at her watch—five, ten, fifteen seconds ticked by before the light changed.

She crossed the intersection and headed for the beach-access path. The sun was just coming up behind her when she arrived at the beach. Ana carefully scanned the horizon, but she saw nothing. As she reached the sand she stopped, took off her shoes and socks, and flung them behind a rock.

She sprinted across the sand, until she reached a boulder close to the pier. Without pausing to catch her breath, she climbed up, sat on top of the rock, and peered out over the ocean. It was the right time of year, and Ana was optimistic. She gazed carefully at the horizon for the telltale spouts but saw nothing. "Patience," she muttered to herself.

"You'll see them; if not today, then tomorrow or next week," Ana repeated to herself as though it were her mantra.

Every December, humpback whales migrated from the frigid waters of Alaska to the tropical climate of Hawaii, where they gave birth to calves and stayed to live in the warm water until it was time to return north. Constantly awestruck by the whales, Ana never tired of watching them leap and frolic in the waves.

She sat on the rock remembering this time last year when she had made a daily pilgrimage to this beach to observe the whales. One day a group of whales had come unusually close to the shore and had entertained her by smacking the water with their tails and occasionally breaching—lifting their entire bodies out of the water and coming down with a resounding whack. She had been alone on the beach that day—a solitary witness to a magnificent performance.

All summer Ana had anticipated whale season, and now that it was finally December, it was time for the first whales to arrive. Although she had come to the beach several times lately, she had not seen a whale yet. Her vision was trained on the horizon.

Watching the water intently, she left her perch and started up the beach to retrieve her shoes. She knew she should hurry, but the waves lapping at her feet were irresistible. She waded a few steps into the surf and stood quietly, feeling the water rushing around her ankles, and at that moment, she saw it.

Off in the distance, a stream of water burst from the surface of the ocean. She waited anxiously to confirm her sighting, and sure enough, it spurted again. The little geysers visible on the horizon were humpback whales spouting. The whales had returned right on schedule. Ana stared into the distance at the amazing creatures before glancing at her watch and quickly scampering home to shower and arrive at school on time.

21. **Which BEST describes the author's tone in the beginning of the story?**

    A   calm

    B   gloomy

    C   urgent

    D   curious

22. **Which sentence from the story is an example of foreshadowing?**

    A   The little geysers visible on the horizon were humpback whales spouting.

    B   She crossed the intersection and headed for the beach-access path.

    C   Ana laced up her running shoes and ran through the kitchen, grabbing a roll from the counter.

    D   Although she had come to the beach several times lately, she had not seen a whale yet.

23. **Read the following from the selection.**

    > Soon, the sun would creep over the mountains and flood her side of the island with light

    In this statement, the author is describing—

    A   the sunrise.

    B   Hawaiian floods.

    C   mountain animals.

    D   the end of the day.

24. **What is the author's purpose in writing this story?**

    A   to present factual information about whales and Hawaiian marine life

    B   to inspire readers to discover the wonders of nature

    C   to entertain readers with a story about a humpback whale

    D   to tell readers a story about different elements of nature in Hawaii

Read the passage below and answer questions 25 through 28.

Sir Duke

Introduction

By the time Duke Ellington published his autobiography *Music is My Mistress* in 1973, he had traveled to dozens of countries and just about every continent. "I pay rent in New York City," he answered when asked of his residence. In the 1920s though, Ellington paid more than rent in New York; he paid his dues on the bandstand. Having moved to Harlem from Washington, D.C. in 1923, Ellington established his own band and achieved critical recognition with a polished sound and appearance. The first New York review of the Ellingtonians in 1923 commented, "The boys look neat in dress suits and labor hard but not in vain at their music." As Ellington made a name for himself as a leader, arranger, and pianist, his Harlem Renaissance compositions and recordings highlighted two enduring characteristics of the artist. Ellington lived for jazz and for Harlem.

The Early Years

Ellington himself admitted he was not a very good pianist as a teenager in Washington. He missed more piano lessons than he took with his teacher Miss Clinkscales, and he spent more time going to dances than practicing the piano. In the clubs, however, Ellington and his friends eventually caught word of New York and the opportunities that awaited young African American musicians there. Ellington wrote, "Harlem, to our minds, did indeed have the world's most glamorous atmosphere. We had to go there." He left Washington with drummer Sonny Greer. They did not enjoy Harlem long before they were penniless. Not until Ellington was fortunate enough to find fifteen dollars on the street could he return to Washington and recollect himself.

Life in Harlem

Ellington eventually did return to Harlem, and he achieved great successes as the bandleader at the Cotton Club from 1927 to 1932. Located in the heart of Harlem at 142nd Street and Lenox Avenue, the Cotton Club was frequented by top entertainers and rich patrons—white and black. Harlem's nightlife, "cut out of a very luxurious, royal-blue bolt of velvet," was an inspirational backdrop, and Ellington composed, arranged, and recorded prolifically to the raves of excited critical acclaim. *Black and Tan Fantasy*, *Hot and Bothered*, and *Rockin' in Rhythm* were Ellington's early hits during this period. They exhibited his unique ability to compose music that animated both dancers in search of a good time and improvising musicians seeking good music. Before long, the once fumbling pianist from Washington, D.C. became the undisputed leader of jazz in Harlem.

25. **According to the passage, the first critical review of the Ellingtonians stated that—**

    A   the musicians were not well-dressed.

    B   Ellington made mistakes in his playing.

    C   the band created a good sound.

    D   Ellington was the leader of a jazz band.

26. **Ellington describes nightlife in Harlem as "cut out of a very luxurious, royal-blue bolt of velvet." The author includes this quote to indicate that the nightlife was—**

    A   extravagant.

    B   fragmented.

    C   ugly.

    D   displeasing.

27. **Read the following from the passage.**

    > Ellington composed, arranged, and recorded prolifically to the raves of excited critical acclaim.

    What does *prolifically* mean?

    A   knowingly

    B   classically

    C   loudly

    D   abundantly

28. **Which of the following strategies does the author use MOST frequently to give a sense of Harlem during the 1920s?**

    A   testimonials

    B   descriptive quotes

    C   song titles

    D   statistics

Read the passage and answer questions 29 through 32.

Capturing the Moment

Eduardo reached slowly into his backpack for his 35-millimeter camera. The herd of wild horses stood warily in the clearing just ahead, sniffing the air loudly and stamping their feet. Eduardo could tell that they knew it was going to rain soon.

Eduardo and his aunt had traveled hundreds of miles to photograph the majestic beauty of this indigenous herd of wild horses. Eduardo's aunt was a freelance photographer. Over the past six months, she had been teaching Eduardo how to take pictures of wild animals in their natural habitats.

The horses tossed their heads impatiently. Eduardo's hands rummaged through his camera bag. He could not take his eyes off of the shimmering manes of the wild horses. The long hairs seemed to catch the light and fall like a handful of rose petals. It was difficult to find his camera in his messy bag with his eyes fixed on the magnificent animals.

"Move very slowly," his aunt cautioned as Eduardo nervously inched forward to get the best shot. She had gracefully removed her camera out and was now taking several photos of the horses. Eduardo had finally pulled the camera from his shoulder bag, and he was now moving closer to set up for his shot.

"These creatures will spook at the slightest snap of a twig," explained Eduardo's aunt in a voice no louder than a whisper.

Though he appreciated his aunt's advice, Eduardo knew the extreme importance of being silent. The previous week, he had read about taking outdoor photos in the most recent issue of *The Snapshot*, a newsletter published by and for young photographers.

Eduardo nodded and smiled back at his aunt. He had been waiting for this moment for a long time; he was not about to make any mistakes now. He brought the camera up to peer through the lens. There was a spotted mare grazing nervously at the edge of the herd, with a small, black foal by her side. The small horse's coat gleamed in the sunlight as the mare raised her head to gently nuzzle him. He turned to gaze—seemingly right at Eduardo—and his stomach dropped as he looked into the foal's large, brown eyes.

He had never seen anything quite so beautiful, and he felt awed by the presence of the young horse. Carefully, so as not to disturb the mare and foal, Eduardo focused his camera. He turned the dial to change the amount of light coming into the lens. Finally, Eduardo snapped a picture. At that moment, the mare's head popped up, and she whinnied a loud warning to the rest of the herd. As if they were one animal, the horses wheeled around and galloped off into the distance. Eduardo lowered his camera and turned to his aunt.

"I don't think I'll ever forget this moment," he sighed. His aunt helped to gather up the camera equipment. Though it was only a brief encounter, Eduardo knew that image would forever be implanted in his memory. He could not wait to develop the film.

29. **The difference between Eduardo's and Eduardo's aunt's initial responses to the wild horses is BEST expressed by which statement?**

  A   He is excited, and she is uninterested

  B   He is tense, and she is calm.

  C   He is professional, and she is amateur.

  D   He is curious, and she is conflicted.

30. **Which statement below is an example of a simile?**

  A   . . . his stomach dropped as he looked into the foal's large, brown eyes.

  B   . . . turned the dial to change the amount of light coming into the lens.

  C   . . . the shimmering manes of the wild horses.

  D   . . . fall like a handful of rose petals.

31. **Which statement below BEST illustrates the time sequence of the events of the story?**

  A   It all takes place on the same day.

  B   It takes place over six months.

  C   It all takes place in two days.

  D   It takes place over a week.

32. **Where does the story take place?**

  A   in a schoolroom

  B   in a park

  C   in a wildlife reserve

  D   in a city zoo

Read this selection and answer questions 33 through 37.

Life with Music

Sunita wore headphones. Before you could even begin to describe how tall she was, or what color hair she had, you had to deal with this important fact. Sunita wore headphones. She took her portable compact-disc player wherever she went. She wore it to school, she wore it in between classes, and she wore it to bed. She even had a waterproof version to wear in the shower.

Sunita loved music. Every paper Sunita wrote for school was about music. She wrote about music for English class by comparing Shakespearean sonnets to her favorite rap lyrics. She wrote about music for Social Studies class by describing the evolution of different musical forms in China. She even found a way to write about music for Science class by comparing the wavelengths of several musical instruments. She studied anything that even remotely touched the world she loved—the world of music.

In the spring of her ninth-grade year, Sunita entered an essay contest sponsored by a prestigious and well-known music camp. She wrote a beautiful and heartfelt essay about the early African American blues artists, and how they had not received the credit that they deserved. Her essay was so powerful and well-written that she won the contest, and Sunita was awarded an entire summer in the mountains studying the thing she loved most.

The music camp was beautiful and serene, nestled in the mountains and far from the noise and chaos of the city where Sunita lived. Of course, Sunita failed to notice this peacefulness; she had her headphones on. She did like going for walks, though—usually just after dinner, before the sun went down.

One evening, she decided to walk along the lakeshore. She clamped her headphones on and set out for a long walk. Soon, she noticed the setting sun. She hopped across a line of large rocks extended into the lake, and she stood on the largest one to watch the sun go down. Unfortunately, the rock was slippery, and Sunita lost her balance, tumbling into the lake.

Sunita, disoriented and scared, thrashed around the lake. The water was deep, and she did not know how to swim very well. Suddenly, she felt a hand grab her and lift her out of the water. She looked up and saw a tall man hauling her to safety.

By the time they reached the shore, a small crowd had gathered. The man had done a heroic deed. People were asking the man if everything was all right. He explained to them what had happened and wrapped a towel around a cold and scared Sunita.

The camp director scolded Sunita for interrupting the man's rehearsal time. Sunita looked again at her rescuer and realized that he was a famous concert pianist who had a house along the lake. "You were practicing?" she asked.

"Yes, I was practicing," the man replied.

"But, but, but. . ." Sunita sputtered. "How did you know I fell in?"

"I heard you," Raolo, the pianist, chuckled.

"But you were playing music."

Raolo picked up Sunita's headphones, "Yes, I was playing. And I was listening to what I was playing. But I could also hear you fall in the water. I could even hear the crickets chirping. I hear them every night. They seem to think I'm accompanying their solo." He laughed and handed Sunita her headphones. "Music is a wonderful part of the world, young lady, but it's not the only part."

The pianist went back inside. Sunita was dragged back to the camp before she could even give back Raolo's towel.

The next day, when her mother heard about her adventure, she offered to send Sunita a new portable CD player and a new pair of headphones to replace the ones that were ruined. Sunita thought about it for a moment, and then said, "Thanks, but maybe later. I've got other things to listen to right now."

33. **Which of the following sentence BEST explains Sunita's biggest problem in the passage?**

    A   She cannot hear the sounds of nature.

    B   She refuses to participate at her music camp.

    C   She has only been able to study subjects related to music.

    D   She is only interested in listening to her headphones.

34. **Which of the following sentences from the story supports the idea that Sunita learned a lesson from the pianist?**

    A   Sunita was dragged back to the camp before she could even give back Raolo's towel.

    B   "Thanks, but maybe later. I've got other things to listen to right now."

    C   "But, but, but. . ." Sunita sputtered. "How did you know I fell in?"

    D   She took her portable compact-disc player wherever she went.

35. **This selection is BEST described as a(n)—**

    A   article.

    B   biography.

    C   story.

    D   play.

36. **Which pair of adjectives BEST describes the mood of this selection?**

    A   satirical, meaningful

    B   reflective, humorous

    C   critical, didactic

    D   solemn, educational

37. **How did Sunita connect her love of music to her academic studies?**

    A   She signed up for extra music classes.

    B   She left school early to go to a music camp.

    C   She listened to her headphones all the time in school.

    D   She incorporated the theme of music into each subject area.

Read this passage and answer questions 38 through 41.

So You Want To Be a Banking Assistant

Welcome to Balloon Financial Partners, Inc. You have been hired as a banking assistant in the Mergers and Acquisitions Department. We're glad to have you aboard!

A banking assistant performs secretarial and administrative services for one or more of our investment bankers. At the analyst level, which is the entry-level position in investment banking, four or five bankers will share an assistant. As a new hire, you will most likely be working with analysts. A banking assistant working for analysts will do basic secretarial work, such as answering telephones and typing documents, but he or she will also perform tasks that are not expected of most secretaries, such as doing corporate research in the library and on the Internet, and compiling information books about companies for whom the firm may be working on a project. Assistants also keep track of bankers' expenses, making sure that they are reimbursed within a reasonable period of time.

As banking assistants work their way up in the firm, they serve fewer and fewer bankers, at higher levels of seniority. Senior banking assistants work for a single managing director or senior vice president. These assistants work very closely with their bankers, setting up meetings and business meals, making travel arrangements, and interfacing with their clients.

We hope your time with Balloon Financial is enriching and successful. Please let us know if there is anything we can do to help you.

The Human Resources Department

Work your way to top pay!

38. **According to the information in the passage, the work of a banking assistant can be summarized BEST by which of the following statements?**

    A client representation

    B investment research

    C meeting coordination

    D administrative support

39. **Which statement from the document BEST support the information in the two boxes?**

    A As banking assistants work their way up in the firm, they serve fewer and fewer bankers. . .

    B We hope your time with Balloon Financial is enriching and successful.

    C At the analyst level, which is the entry-level position in investment banking. . .

    D . . . he or she will also perform tasks that are not expected of most secretaries, such as doing corporate research in the library and on the Internet. . .

40. **What is the purpose of this selection?**

    A to inform employees of changes in company policies

    B to introduce new employees to their position

    C to explain the structure of the firm

    D to request a new procedure for hiring banking assistants

41. **From the information in the passage, one can conclude that banking assistants—**

    A act as low-level investment analysts.

    B revise written draft mergers for clients.

    C aid bankers in all aspects of their work.

    D maintain bankers' personal correspondence.

Read the essay and answer questions 42 through 45.

To Measure His Success

What does it mean to be "successful?" Do we measure success by money? By possessions? By celebrity? If I told you about a man who worked as a teacher, a land surveyor, and in a pencil factory and never held any of these jobs for more than a few years, would that man sound like a success to you? If I told you that he spent two years living alone in a small cabin that he built for himself, and that he spent those years looking at plants and writing in a diary, would you think of him as a celebrity or an important figure? What if I told you that he rarely ventured far from the town where he was born, that he was thrown in jail for refusing to pay his taxes, and that he died at the age of forty-five? Do any of these facts seem to point to a man whose life should be studied and emulated?

You may already know about this man. You may even have read some of his writings. His name was Henry David Thoreau, and he was, in addition to the jobs listed above, a poet, an essayist, a naturalist, and a social critic. Although the facts listed about him may not seem to add up to much, he was, in fact, a tremendously influential person. Along with other writers such as Ralph Waldo Emerson, Mark Twain, and Walt Whitman, Thoreau helped to create the first literature and philosophy that most people identify as distinct voice from the United States.

Thoreau was born in Concord, Massachusetts, in 1817, and Concord remained the center and focus of his life. As a young man, he worked as a teacher at several different schools. Before he even graduated from college, he contracted tuberculosis, a disease that plagued him throughout his life and eventually led to his death.

Thoreau became a close friend of the author Ralph Waldo Emerson, and he lived with the Emerson family for three years, earning his keep as a handyman. Thoreau and Emerson saw the world similarly, and together they became the chief proponents of the new philosophy of Transcendentalism. This philosophy held that the divine spirit was alive in humans and nature, and that individual intuition was the highest source of knowledge.

In 1845, Thoreau built a cabin on Walden Pond, near Concord, and remained there for more than two years, living alone, fending for himself, and observing the nature around him. He kept scrupulous notes in his diary, notes that he later distilled into his most famous work, *Walden*. Early in that book, Thoreau explained the purpose behind his retreat from society:

I went to the woods because I wished to live deliberately, to front only the essential facts of life, and see if I could not learn what it had to teach, and not, when I came to die, discover that I had not lived. I wanted to live deep and suck out all the marrow of life, to put to rout all that was not life.

Thoreau was a firm believer in the abolition of slavery, and he objected to the practice's extension into the new territories of the West. To protest this practice, and the U.S.-Mexican War that was encouraging it, Thoreau publicly and vocally refused to pay his taxes in 1846. For this act of rebellion, he was thrown in the Concord jail. He spent only a night there, as his friend Emerson came to bail him out.

Thoreau used his writing to spread his message of resistance and activism. In 1849, he published an essay entitled "Civil Disobedience" (also known as "Resistance to Civil Government"). In it, Thoreau laid out his argument for refusing to obey unjust laws:

The only obligation [that] I have a right to assume is to do what I think right. There are thousands who are in opinion opposed to slavery and to the war, who do nothing to put an end to them. If one thousand, if one hundred, if ten men whom I could name—if ten honest men only—aye, if one HONEST man, in this State of Massachusetts, ceasing to hold slaves, were actually to withdraw from this partnership, and be locked up in the county jail for it, it would be the abolition of slavery in America. For it matters not how small the beginning may seem to be: what is once well done is done forever.

This essay may have had the most lasting impact of anything Thoreau wrote. Although it did not by itself end enslavement in the United States, it influenced many in the Abolition Movement. The essay continued to influence men and women in future generations. Mahatma Gandhi based some of his ideas of non-violent protest on Thoreau's essay; as did Dr. Martin Luther King, Jr.; the student protesters against the Vietnam War; and democracy protesters in China and the Soviet Union.

It is impossible to know what influence Thoreau might have had on his own generation, had illness not cut his life short.

Thoreau's life was brief, his works and his ideas continue to touch and influence people. Students all over the country—all over the world—continue to read his essays and hear his unique voice, urging them to lead lives of principle, individuality, and freedom.

To be able to live out, so forcefully and fully, the ideas that burn in one's heart—and to have those ideas touch other hearts in distant times and lands— surely, that is the meaning of success.

42. In which of the following statements from the passage does the author set up a sense of irony about Thoreau's accomplishments?

   A Mahatma Gandhi based some of his ideas of non-violent protest on Thoreau's essay. . .

   B If I told you about a man who worked as a teacher, a land surveyor, and in a pencil factory and never held any of these jobs for more than a few years, would that man sound like a success to you?

   C Thoreau was born in Concord, Massachusetts, in 1817, and Concord remained the center and focus of his life.

   D . . . in addition to the jobs listed above, a poet, an essayist, a naturalist, and a social critic.

43. Which of the following sentences from the passage BEST reflects the author's attitude toward Thoreau?

   A Before he even graduated from college, he contracted tuberculosis, a disease that plagued him throughout his life and eventually led to his death.

   B Although the facts listed about him may not seem to add up to much, he was, in fact, a tremendously influential person.

   C Do any of these facts seem to point to a man whose life should be studied and emulated?

   D Thoreau and Emerson saw the world similarly, and together they became the chief proponents of the new philosophy of Transcendentalism.

44. How did Thoreau respond to the events in the United States during his lifetime?

   A He went to jail to prove that his perspective was right.

   B He preferred to stay in his town in Massachusetts.

   C He recorded the events and viewpoints of the period.

   D He used his words to try to change what he saw as unfair.

45. The main idea of Thoreau's "Civil Disobedience" is that—

   A people have the right to do whatever they want whenever they want.

   B people in Massachusetts should stop participating in the enslavement system.

   C citizens should not have to obey laws that are unjust.

   D citizens should not have to pay taxes if they do not want to.

Session 2

The following is a rough draft of an essay discussing two pieces of literature. It may contain errors in grammar, punctuation, sentence structure, and capitalization. Some of the questions may refer to underlined or numbered sentences or phrases within the text. Read the essay and answer questions 46 through 50.

Roxanna and Astrid: Voices that Become Our Own

(1) Reynolds Price pries open the inner workings of an ordinary Southern woman born in 1900. (2) Now in her nineties, Roxanna recalls the events that shaped her life. (3) Only one was unusual, but it set the course for all others. (4) Roxanna, on an extraordinary afternoon in her youth, she falls in love with a handsome young man who she's been sent to meet him for a possible marriage. (5) Within hours he unexpectedly drowns before her eyes, and Roxanna later goes on to wed his brother. (6) Nothing dramatic occurs again, but Roxanna's straightforward, practical retelling lulls us direct towards her experiences.

(7) Astrid Magnussen of Janet Fitch's *White Oleander* is equally unheroic. (8) Fitch, like Price, creates a distinct voice for her character. (9) Without self-pity, Astrid explores different ways to survive—making emotional alliances that might make readers uneasy. (10) But we see the world through her adolescent eyes. (11) We come to understand why Astrid does what she does.

(12) The personal narratives <u>in these novels transport us</u> not just to different times and places, but also into the actual lives of seemingly real people. (13) If told objectively, little happens in these books that would grab our attention. (14) But the characters' voices allow their inner most experiences to become our own.

46. **Which sentence would BEST begin the essay?**

    A   The writers Janet Fitch and Reynolds Price used their compelling characters to draw readers in.

    B   I am going to write about two writers named Reynolds Price and Janet Fitch.

    C   Most readers appreciate well-written characters.

    D   Authors Janet Fitch and Reynolds Price have some interesting things happen to their characters.

47. **Which phrase would BEST replace the phrase "direct towards" in the sentence labeled 6?**

    A   directedly to

    B   directly into

    C   directions to

    D   direct in two

48. **What is the BEST way to combine the sentences labeled 10 and 11?**

    A   But we see the world through her adolescent eyes, or we come to understand why Astrid does what she does.

    B   But we see the world through her adolescent eyes, because we come to understand why Astrid does what she does.

    C   But we see the world through her adolescent eyes, and we come to understand why Astrid does what she does.

    D   But we see the world through her adolescent eyes, if we come to understand why Astrid does what she does.

49. **Which is the MOST effective substitution for the underlined part of sentence 12?**

    A   in these novels transporting us

    B   in these novels transports us

    C   in these novels would transport us

    D   Leave as is.

50. **Which of the following ideas is supported by details or evidence in the essay?**

    A   Reynolds Price and Janet Fitch are writers in their nineties.

    B   Astrid is the heroine of Janet Fitch's *White Oleander*.

    C   Reynolds Price uses uncomplicated language to tell the story of her characters.

    D   Janet Fitch and Reynolds Price both wrote about characters named Astrid.

The following passage is a rough draft. It may contain errors in grammar, punctuation, sentence structure, or organization. Read the passage and answer questions 51 through 55.

My Job Interview

(1) Kamal is my best friend. (2) He works at a seafood restaurant and recommended me to his manager. (3) There <u>was a job opening</u> in the restaurant. (4) I immediately went to the restaurant to pick up an application. (5) I had been looking for a job for a long time since we were off from school. (6) The opportunity was too good to be missed. (7) I knew that I could make a good impression.

(8) I was careful when I filled out my application. (9) I triple checked it for errors. (10) I was both excited and nervous when I received a phone call from the manager. (11) "Would you," she asked, "like to schedule a time for an interview?" (12) I happily responded and set up an interview with her.

(13) I went to the interview looking my best. (14) I spent the morning picking out my clothes and ironing them. (15) Even though I felt very nervous, I <u>acted powerfully and graciously</u>. (16) The manager, Carol, was responsive and put my mind at ease immediately. (17) She started by reviewing my application. (18) I learned during the interview that I was well-suited to the job. (19) I hoped that the manager recognized my great interest. (20) I went home to treat myself to ice cream.

(21) Later that night, Kamal called me to ask me about the interview. (22) "So, how did you feel about the interview, Ayala?"

(23) "Kamal, I felt very prepared. (24) We'll have to see what happens next!"

51. **Which is the MOST effective substitution for the underlined part of sentence 3?**

    A   are a job opening

    B   is a opening

    C   were an opening

    D   Leave as is.

52. **Which of the following sentences does NOT fit well in the paragraph in which it is found?**

    A   He works at a seafood restaurant and recommended me to his manager. (first paragraph)

    B   I triple checked it for errors. (second paragraph)

    C   I went home to treat myself to ice cream. (third paragraph)

    D   We'll have to see what happens next! (fourth paragraph)

53. **What is the BEST way to write sentence 11?**

    A   "Would you like to schedule a time for an interview? she asked."

    B   "Would you like to schedule a time for an interview?" she asked.

    C   "Would you like to schedule a time for an interview," she asked?

    D   Leave as is.

54. **In order to achieve more precise meaning, the underlined phrase in sentence 15 should be changed to—**

    A   felt mean.

    B   was confident.

    C   said specific things.

    D   talked with weakness.

55. **Which of the following ideas is supported by details or evidence in the passage?**

    A   Kamal is a thoughtful and caring friend.

    B   Ayala had never been to a job interview before.

    C   Carol will probably not give Ayala the position.

    D   Ayala wore new clothes to her interview.

The following is a rough draft of an essay discussing the invention of written alphabets. The essay may contain errors in grammar, punctuation, sentence structure, and capitalization. Some of the questions may refer to underlined or numbered sentences or phrases within the text. Read the essay and answer questions 56 through 60.

The Written Alphabet

Everyone talks about the "global village," but there couldn't be a global village today if there hadn't been smaller villages many years ago, and then (1) towns, and then countries. Although the human race began as one people, we spread all over the planet and lost touch with each other. Little by little, over the years, humans began reaching out to each other over greater and greater distances. And none of it could have happened without the alphabet.

Modern life as we know it would be unthinkable without a written language, and a written language is impossible without an alphabet. Written language makes it possible for us to communicate with large numbers of people at once, in a clear and consistent way. Music also allows people to communicate with each other. With hieroglyphic languages, people needed to know what ideas your symbols represent. Outside of your own little community, people would have a hard time understanding your symbols, because those symbols will be closely related to your community and your (2) life. This limited the ability of different peoples to communicate.

With an alphabet, the language can be clear and comprehensible wherever it's read, no matter who reads it. This has allowed ideas and cultures to happen all over the world. We could not have anything like the Internet (3) today if we didn't have a written alphabet that people all over the world could read. Perhaps now, after spreading all over the earth, we are finally, slowly, becoming one people again.

56. What is the BEST way to express the ideas in the sentence labeled (1)?

A   Everyone talks about the "global village," but there couldn't be a global village today. If there hadn't been smaller villages many years ago, and then towns, and then countries.

B   Everyone talks about the "global village," but there couldn't be a global village today if there hadn't been smaller villages many years ago. And then towns, and then countries.

C   Everyone talks about the global village but there couldn't be a global village today if there hadn't been smaller villages many years ago, and then towns, and then countries.

D   Leave as is.

57. Which of the following would be the MOST precise way to state the underlined words labeled (2)?

A   those symbols had been closely related

B   those symbols are closely related

C   those symbols would be closely related

D   Leave as is.

58. In order to achieve more precise meaning, the underlined word labeled (3) should be changed to—

A   grow and spread.

B   shrink and disappear.

C   clash and conflict.

D   Leave as is.

59. Which of the following sentences does NOT fit well in the paragraph in which it is found?

A   "Although the human race began as one people, we spread all over the planet and lost touch with each other." (first paragraph)

B   "Music also allows people to communicate with each other." (second paragraph)

C   "This limited the ability of different peoples to communicate." (second paragraph)

D   "Perhaps now, after spreading all over the earth, we are finally, slowly, becoming one people again." (third paragraph)

60. What source is BEST for finding out information about written alphabets used in Ghana, West Africa?

A   a play about African languages

B   an encyclopedia article about Ghana

C   a book about written languages

D   a chapter on African geography

For questions 61 through 66, choose the answer that is the most effective substitute for each underlined part of the sentence. If no substitution is necessary, choose "Leave as is."

61. <u>They arrived at the Gulf;</u> and boarded Celia's parents' sailboat.

   A   They arrived at the Gulf

   B   They arrived at the Gulf,

   C   They arrived at the Gulf:

   D   Leave as is.

62. <u>"Where is Michelle?" my mother asked.</u>

   A   "Where is Michelle"? my mother asked.

   B   "Where is Michelle" my mother asked.

   C   "Where is Michelle," my mother asked?

   D   Leave as is.

63. In 1917, Gideon Sundback patented a type of sliding fastener that resembled the modern zipper. <u>The U.S. Navy used these early zippers. The Navy used them in flying suits during World War I.</u>

   A   Using these early zippers, the Navy used them in flying suits during World War I.

   B   The U.S. Navy used these early zippers in flying suits during World War I.

   C   In flying suits during World War I; the U.S. Navy used these early zippers.

   D   Leave as is.

64. <u>Me and my friends</u> LaKeisha and Kwame like to spend time at the beach in the summer.

   A   I and my friends

   B   My friends and me

   C   My friends and I

   D   Leave as is.

65. People in the United States eat more ice cream than do people in any other country. <u>The most popular flavor is vanilla, the second most popular flavor is chocolate.</u>

   A   The most popular flavor is vanilla, chocolate is the second most popular flavor.

   B   The most popular flavor is vanilla and the second most popular flavor is chocolate.

   C   The most popular flavor is vanilla; the second most popular flavor is chocolate.

   D   Leave as is.

66. Important math skills include counting, measuring, and <u>perform a variety of functions.</u>

   A   performing a variety of functions.

   B   knowing how a variety of functions are performed.

   C   functioning a variety of things.

   D   Leave as is.

For questions 67 through 72, choose the word or phrase that best completes the sentence.

67. Noelia was _____ forward to an afternoon away from loud campers.

   A   looks

   B   look

   C   looking

   D   looked

68. Of all the sports in the world, rugby is by far my _____.

   A   favoritest

   B   most favorite

   C   more favorite

   D   favoriter

69. Neither Lincoln nor Roosevelt _____ uncritical acceptance during their lifetimes.

   A   enjoy

   B   enjoys

   C   enjoyed

   D   would have enjoyed

70. Jorge opened the closet door slowly and _____ that Cloretta was hiding inside.

   A   carefully; he knew

   B   carefully but he knew

   C   carefully, he knew

   D   carefully he knew

71. "Are you _____ the inspector asked dryly, "that a terrible crime has just been committed?"

   A   aware,

   B   aware"

   C   aware?"

   D   aware,"

72. Neither my teacher, my mother, nor I _____ any idea what you are talking about.

   A   have

   B   had

   C   having

   D   haves

73. Writing Task

REMINDER

- Write your response to the writing prompt below.
- You may NOT use a dictionary. If you do not know how to spell a word, sound the word out and do the best you can.
- You may either print or write in cursive.
- Write clearly! Any erasures or strike-throughs should be as clean as possible.

WRITING TASK:

   Your school has announced that it will terminate all music and drama programming citing that these programs distract students from their school work.

   Write a business letter to your school administration in which you convince the readers of the importance of keeping music and drama programming. Convince your readers through the use of specific reasons and examples.

Checklist for Your Writing

The following checklist will help you do your best work. Make sure you:

- ☐ Read the description of the task carefully.
- ☐ Organize your writing with a strong introduction, body, and conclusion.
- ☐ State your position and support it with specific examples.
- ☐ Choose a style, tone, and vocabulary that are appropriate for your audience and purpose.
- ☐ Vary your sentences to make your writing interesting to read.
- ☐ Check for mistakes in grammar, spelling, punctuation, capitalization, and sentence structure.

Name _____   Date _____

_____

_____

_____

_____

_____

_____

_____

_____

_____

_____

_____

_____

_____

_____

_____

_____

_____

_____

_____

_____

_____

_____

_____

_____

_____

_____

_____

_____

_____

_____

_____

_____

_____

_____

_____

_____

_____

_____

_____

_____

_____

_____

_____

_____

_____

_____

_____

_____

_____

_____

NOTES

NOTES

NOTES

NOTES

NOTES